A Little Bouquet

A Little Bouquet

SELECTED WORKS OF
GERALDINE CLINTON LITTLE

EDITED BY AMANDA FIELD

CREATIVE ARTS BOOK COMPANY
BERKELEY, CA
2001

Cover design: Ingalls + Associates, San Francisco

Cover painting: Gary Bukovnik

For information contact:
Creative Arts Book Company
833 Bancroft Way
Berkeley, CA 94710

ISBN 088739-433-7
Library of Congress Catalog Number 2001092799

Printed in the United States of America

To all the flowers and petals in
Geraldine Clinton Little's rich bouquet:
Bob.
Rory, Tim, and Rod.
Matthew Clinton-Lee, Robert James, Justin Trevor,
Patrick Clinton, Andrea Geraldine.
The Harmony Five: Gwen, Trevor, Kenneth, Ailsa, Hilda (Moira).
Mama, Dada, and Ninny.
Uncle Howard, Uncle Charlie,
Kay & Bob Peterson, Hiro Sato,
and unnamed friends, loves, and inspirations.

CONTENTS

PREFACE

My mother always advised that a writer should strive to eliminate adjectives. But in remembering her, a flood of adjectives cascades upon me: Remarkable. Creative. Sensitive. Combative. Polite (unfailingly; even irritatingly). Strong. Insecure. Energetic. Independent. Lovely. Loving. Whimsical. Worldly. Naïve. Sensuous. Curious. Complicated. I am not sure I've ever known anyone that inspired as many adjectives as does the memory of Geraldine Clinton Little.

This book, patiently nurtured by Howard Junker, editor of *ZYZZYVA* magazine, and edited with great finesse by Amanda Field, is a tribute to the breadth and diversity of my mother's work. While not beginning her career as serious writer until an age at which many contemplate retirement, my mother produced poems, haiku, short stories, and nonfiction at a prodigious pace right up until the month she died. Even then, she left three unpublished manuscripts, with instructions.

My brothers, Timothy Howard Little and Rodney Clinton Little, have joined me in supporting this volume, not only as a memorial to our mother and a resource for her friends and family, but also as a legacy for our children. (The remembrances that follow, however, are largely mine; my brothers bear no responsibility for error or offense.) We also think she was an exceptional poet and writer, whose work merits study and review.

Geraldine Frances Clinton was born in 1923 in Portstewart, Northern Ireland, on the edge of the sea 50 miles northwest of Belfast. The youngest by seven years of six children, she was an "afterthought" to her two brothers and three sisters. Together with grandparents and a maiden aunt, this large family lived on the meager salary of an itinerant Methodist minister, who was moved by his church to a new parish every two years.

The Reverend James Robert Clinton, her father, was a proud and strict taskmaster, towering above the family figuratively as well as literally at over six feet. His wife, Louisa Margaret Corr, had been well educated at the London College of Music. Together with Ninny (Louisa's sister), the Clintons shepherded a talented and disciplined group of children into long, creative, and independent lives. Each child, for example, was required to learn to play the piano and one other instrument, as well as to sing in the church choir. Each continued into adulthood to perform in various professional groups and settings across the country. My mother's sister Ailsa became a well-known harpist in the Los Angeles area, and her sister Hilda sang with the Baltimore Symphony Chorus. My mother as well sang professionally, with the Philadelphia Orchestra in the Mendelssohn Club and later the Choral Arts Society, until she was 72.

Making a living was not easy in Northern Ireland in the 1920s. Chasing economic security, Dr. Clinton and his wife left for the United States in 1924, very soon after my mother's birth. Ninny and Grandma Corr stayed to care for the children, and not until May 1925 did the extended family set sail for New York, a nine-day adventure. My mother's oldest sister, Gwen, recalled that they traveled with 32 suitcases, after selling or giving away many of their possessions.

After a few months in Broad Channel, Long Island, the Clinton clan settled in Philadelphia, where my grandfather accepted the pastorate of the Central Congregationalist Church. The family quickly formed the "Harmony Five," hiring themselves out to churches and religious meetings. The five oldest children would sing, with Mrs. Clinton (who died in 1950 before I was born) providing accompaniment on the organ. Dr. Clinton would offer a rousing sermon. Quite a bargain was the Clinton family.

Brought up strictly in this close and musical, but never prosperous, family, my mother went off to college at 18—to Tusculum, a small Presbyterian college in Tennessee, far from her parents' supervisory eyes. But the family could not afford this luxury, and after only a year she had to return home. Yet the experience was life-altering: she met Kay, who together with the Reverend Bob Peterson, the man Kay later married, remained my mother's closest friends to the end of her life.

Upon her return to Philadelphia, the vivacious and always independent Gerrie Clinton quickly found work in various executive secretary jobs. Such was the lot of an intelligent woman in the 1940s: helping men run their businesses.

By the time she was 23, my mother had saved enough to travel back to Ireland. Gwen and her husband—my "Uncle Charliehorse"— and their children saw her off at La Guardia Airport. She often spoke of this courageous journey with pride and delight, having gone by herself in an era when it was not common for a young woman to travel alone.

Family legend tells that she met my father in a Philadelphia apartment building elevator in the early 1950s. A group of young people in this building enjoyed staging amateur theatricals. My mother was in the cast, and my father helped build the sets—more to meet women, we always suspected, than for any particular love of drama. They married when she was 30, in that time on the perceived brink of spinsterhood. She had turned down other offers; my father's practical nature and playful enthusiasm for life provided a spark unique among the arts set in which my mother traveled.

Little did she know that my father would call upon her to live far from the lights of the city. Trained as an engineer, my father longed to pursue his own inventions. Three months after I was born in 1956, he quit his job as an industrial sales representative and started his own company. Seeking affordable industrial space, he and my mother moved to a small town in the wilds of South Jersey where they knew no one, but new houses were affordable and a corner of a warehouse was available for his startup.

Mount Holly is known to some as the hometown of NFL stars Franco Harris and Irving Fryar. But the town predates the Revolutionary War and is the site of a number of historic homes, as well as the Burlington County seat. Part of Mount Holly's charm has always been that it lies on the edge of that vast pygmy forest called the Pine Barrens, and is bisected by a lovely, meandering creek known as the Rancocas. Although my mother sometimes lamented the unsophisticated character of "little ole Mount Holly," thirty miles distant over then-two-lane roads from the cultural institutions of Philadelphia, she came to love its greenery, comfortable pace, and easy access to the lovely South Jersey Shore. Her poetry captures her love of the beautiful and diverse natural environs that South Jersey offers, still a relatively well-kept secret.

The new tract neighborhood my parents moved into in the winter of 1956 lacked paved roads; old home-movies show an expanse of rainy mud. The two small children's bedrooms on Bong Terrace were soon bursting with three Little boys. Then one Saturday (again the family legend) my father came home and announced that he'd bought a larger place. 519 Jacksonville Road was a sprawling eighteenth-century farmhouse and barn on two acres (!) right in the middle of town next to the local elementary and high schools. (We always walked to school, a luxury that seems even greater in retrospect.)

My mother always claimed that Dad had bought the place one weekend without consulting her. This seems likely, as the house was relatively dilapidated when we moved in. A dirt driveway led from the street to the house, the "Barn" (now a garage) had stables just a few years short of horses, and the house contained ancient plumbing, heating, and electrical systems that only a mechanic could love. But like many things my father provided us, this huge place—four stories with over 20 rooms (although a number were unfinished), fruit trees and a large open field out back—became inseparably connected to family warmth as we grew up and out. It also became the neighborhood recreation center for all our childhood friends. Typical of my parents' unspoken efforts to keep their children out of trouble was the tennis/basketball court that my father later built by himself in the back field. Although it was slightly below professional standards— the unsurfaced asphalt would turn a tennis ball black within ten minutes—we often played until 11 p.m. under bright lights he mounted on 30-foot poles. How my father avoided the wrath of his neighbors we never knew, nor did we even think to ask.

This oddball house, in an isolated town, symbolizes for me the loneliness of writing. For 28 years, my mother steadily typed on her manual typewriter in a tiny upstairs sitting room she turned into her office. Yet in the end, none of us would have traded any of this— Mount Holly, the odd house, the distance from city life—for the world. Indeed, my mother refused to leave the house even once she was alone and her health steadily declined. She spent her final hours resting on a rented hospital bed in the formal dining room where she had entertained for 36 years.

My mother, who had not been keen on abandoning Philadelphia, made the most of her opportunities in a small town. She sang as a paid soloist for the Mount Holly Presbyterian Church and for other local congregations, and then regularly with the more professional Moorestown Presbyterian choir one town over—again, until only months before she died. The classical music station was always on, and my father installed hidden speakers—years ahead of his time, as usual—so that music could be heard throughout the house. Every Saturday afternoon my two younger brothers and I were compelled to hear the Metropolitan Opera on the radio "live from New York," to the unending amusement of our friends.

Made to don coat and tie, we often journeyed to hear the Philadelphia Orchestra and see exhibitions at the Museum of Art. By the age of seven, we had memorized the science exhibits at the Franklin Institute (the giant heart being our favorite, of course). When we were eleven, nine, and seven, my mother organized a three-week adventure to England, Scotland, and Ireland, quite an unusual trip among our Mount Holly classmates. We were compelled to take piano lessons for years, although none of us can now play more than *Chopsticks*. Later, we dutifully marched to literary readings. Of course, we hated the formality of all of this. But today each of us has an appreciation for music and the arts for which we are grateful. My mother is responsible for this. She did not simply pursue art for herself, but continually pushed it out into the unwashed world (and vice versa).

Of course, my mother was a proud eccentric. Throughout our years at home, she would flit around the house singing snatches of opera or choir music, generally to our embarrassment. Shy in initial conversations, she wore outrageously showy jewelry, rings on many fingers, perhaps as compensation.

My father's eccentricity was both contrast and complement to my mother's. He unfailingly wore a bow tie in the 1970s, when it was simply a crazy departure, not political style. Most of our friends still have one of the silver dollars he palmed to visitors every Christmas season. "Rodney, go elsewhere" is a rather unexpected phrase that shall live, among a select group of my friends, in my father's voice forever.

Yet while both fiercely independent, my parents were far from twin souls. As just one example, the memory of listening to my mother, a proud member of Another Mother For Peace, arguing with my father, who defended Richard Nixon to the end, about whether I would go to Vietnam or Canada in 1973 is clear, although I felt oddly unconnected to it at the time. (When the draft ended just before I turned 18, no choice was required.) And while my father dutifully attended church, symphony, and literary events, particularly if my mother was performing, he might on occasion be caught napping in the back row.

My mother's energy always overflowed. She was impatient with actionless criticism. If the elementary school lacked a decent library, well then, she would become librarian (and later president of the PTA). If Mount Holly lacked cultural amenities, she would create some. She was instrumental in transforming the Mount Holly library from a somewhat rundown place into a respectable educational resource. She helped found and was president of the Burlington County chapter of Community Concerts, a national organization that helped small towns import world-class musicians. Later, she routinely gave readings and taught poetry and literature classes at all the local schools.

Meanwhile, my father's fortunes slowly improved as he developed his own patented invention, the pinch valve, which was a new way to control the flow of liquids in any size of pipe. With no funds to manufacture a working demonstrator, he built one of wood, spray-painted it silver to look like metal, and obtained his first contracts based on photographs and speculation. Over time, his invention became the industry standard and his company prospered. "RKL Controls, the World's Largest Manufacturer of Pinch Valves." We need not mention that it was, for a time, the only manufacturer. (My father's initials, RKL, are mine, although I inherited none of his mechanical genius. He was quietly disappointed that none of his sons wanted to inherit his business, which he finally sold in 1980.) Ultimately, my father held over 20 patents. Yet in the first years, until he could afford a secretary, my mother handled all the finances, contracts, and correspondence. Her inclinations may have run to the arts, but she had been trained as an executive secretary and she knew how to run a business.

By the 1960s, my father's rented warehouse gave way to a larger manufacturing plant in Hainesport, New Jersey. Ultimately, RKL Controls moved to the largest solar-heated-and-cooled industrial building in the United States, which my father designed and built on a federal grant favoring this new technology. Never did the dreams and ambitions of my parents have limits. Another valuable trait conveyed to their sons.

When my youngest brother, Rodney, started school, my mother decided to complete her college degree at last. She enrolled at Goddard College in Vermont, a gem of a small college that fosters individual creativity. Goddard helped her design a course of study performed largely by correspondence, requiring residence only a few weeks each semester. We learned to ski (badly) at Stowe during her winter residences. She was a straight-A student, and had difficulty understanding how her children could occasionally seem to squander educational opportunities that she, child of the Depression, considered pure privilege.

Our educations proceeded in a strangely linked way. I recall studying for my biology exam in the tenth grade at the same time she was studying for hers at Goddard. We were proud, if a bit bemused, to attend her college graduation while we were teenagers. But my mother quickly pushed on, obtaining her master's degree in English literature from Trenton State and taking other graduate courses well into her later years. We always thought it odd when, every September, she would tell us how she always looked forward to the beginning of a new school year. But my mother was a born student and simply loved the enterprise of learning. This intellectual curiosity pervades her poetry; she studied history, science, and nature deeply before she would write sonnets touching on the topics.

What led my mother to begin writing for publication at the age of 45? In a word, she had a cancer scare. While hospitalized in the late 1960s for a biopsy, which fortunately proved negative, she confronted her own mortality and decided she would no longer dabble in the private notebooks she had kept since girlhood. She wrote a somewhat maudlin account of her cancer experience and her love of her young family, and McCall's magazine bought it for $300! That was a huge sum of money to her—and it was her own money, not her husband's. From that moment on, she actively pursued publication.

Invoking Walt Whitman, she initially self-published. As she became better known, she was published by others. Her nom de plume vacillated between "Geraldine Clinton" and "Geraldine Clinton Little"; she was never quite sure if she should be her own woman or embrace her married, familial status, although after my father died in 1990, the "Little" became permanent.

My mother always wanted to be published in *The New Yorker*. But she never was, though she sent them many poems. Indeed, rejection, she always told us, was part of a poet's existence. After her death, I found a file of rejection letters six inches thick. But there were also many acceptances, and the various magazines and journals that published her poetry fill many boxes. Over a quarter century, her poems, short fiction, and articles appeared in about 300 journals.

Her literary accomplishments extended beyond publication. She served as president of the Haiku Society of America. She was a vice-president of the Poetry Society of America. She taught at countless writers' conferences. She was a writer-in-residence at the prestigious artists' retreat, Yaddo, and was a fellow of the MacDowell Colony. She was the recipient of at least two grants from the New Jersey Arts Council and received over a dozen writers' awards. Into her seventies, she organized poetry seminars and lectures throughout the Delaware Valley. She led an annual haiku workshop and competition at the local junior high. She even established her own poetry press, Silver Apples, which emphasized first collections. It is to honor this vision that my brothers and I have endowed in her memory the Poetry Society of America's William Carlos Williams Prize for a first book of poetry, as well as the publication of three first books of poetry by *ZYZZYVA*.

Throughout, my mother maintained a steady teaching income as an adjunct professor at the nearby Burlington County (then-Community) College, as well as occasional teaching engagements at Trenton State College and Rutgers. Her play, *Heloise and Abelard,* was produced at Burlington County (as well as off-Broadway in New York), and the College has named its theater in her honor. Hers was a teaching career of extremes: advanced literature and poetry for top students, as well as seventh-grade poetry seminars and remedial English for adults. (And if the weight of the stories she told is any indication, her greatest fulfillment came from the latter. My mother always passionately favored the underdog.)

Whenever Geraldine Little's sons feel that they have too much to do, we remember our mother and her seemingly inexhaustible reserves of energy for diverse, worthwhile activities. Our father, too, was cut from this same over-committed cloth: president of the Rotary Club, the YMCA, and Junior Achievement, all while running his own business. My mother's insistent "Don't just sit there, go out and do something!" still rings in my ears. Independence and constant activity—it is both our blessing and our curse.

Every day of her mature life, my mother would write in a tiny, unheated room that hung out over our driveway and had windows on three sides. It was a bright and contemplative room, and she was fond of the muted sounds of children playing on the neighboring elementary school playground. She worked hard and always told us that writing was a discipline you could not relax. "I would like to dispel the notion that you sit down and wait for the moonlight to stream over your pen," she once told a reporter. "There is an enormous amount of craft to poetry."

My mother's other favorite place was the kitchen, which had a window that looked out on oak and pine trees and her garden. She would often delight in the sight of a squirrel scurrying up a tree or blue jays feeding at her well-stocked feeder. She loved to take walks on "the Mount" in Mount Holly or in the neighborhood with our various dogs. After my brothers and I left home, she and my father would often drive to Maine on the spur of the moment, and take meandering, unplanned jaunts through the countryside and coastal towns.

Geraldine Clinton Little's writing is as multifaceted as her own character. What follows reveals a keen eye for nature's details, a love of the natural and spiritual worlds, a commitment to social justice and particularly women's issues, an honoring of history and its indispensable personalities, and a longing for peacefulness. It well displays, but does not capture, her soul.

One night in October 1990, my father died without warning. My mother, on the other hand, knew she was dying for six months or more. She wrote ever more feverishly when she realized that her own death was truly at hand, and left careful instructions regarding her unpublished manuscripts (two of which were published posthumously by her own deathbed efforts). On February 6, 1997, her fifth grandchild, Andrea Geraldine Little, was born. Four weeks later, my wife took our daughter to visit "Nana," and on the evening of March 6 my mother sat in her sickbed and lovingly held Andrea in her arms for over an hour. That night she died with my brother Tim at her side. Too soon, and unwillingly—still more to do!—but in the glow of a full and remarkable life. We love her still.

Rory Little
San Francisco, June 2001

EDITOR'S NOTE

Geraldine Clinton Little published eight books of poetry, eight chapbooks, one book of short stories, a book of essays, and a verse play. She also left two book-length manuscripts unpublished at her death. She was a contributor to an anthology of New Jersey writers that also included Joyce Carol Oates and Amiri Baraka. She served as president of the Haiku Society of America and as vice-president of the Poetry Society of America. In making the selections for this volume, I have tried to capture the range and complexity of her career.

Part I gathers together early reminiscences. Some of these are nonfiction memoir; others are fictional, though steeped in autobiography. Whether recollected or imagined, these stories and poems attest to her unfailing devotion to her family.

Part II is a testament to her sense of the natural world as a source of delight and wonderment. Again and again, she finds in nature something akin to what her deeply devout parents found in religion:

> I whisper denial,
> deny the high throne of His sky
> but affirm my place
> on earth, its muddy stench,
> its rutting masses, those mysteries
> sufficient for a lifetime's labor.

Part III through Part VII illustrate her dedication to social issues. She was acutely aware that the contributions of women often went unheralded, and, to redress this historical imbalance, she wrote many dramatic monologues in the personae of historical figures—women such as Mussolini's mistress Ida Dalser, Revolutionary War heroine Molly Pitcher, and poet Anne Sexton. A selection of these comprise Part III. She writes, "I was drawn to writing about the lives of women, for women so often sublimate their needs and dreams to the demands of others.... I was moved to attempt to retrieve some who have been relegated to footnotes or only a page or two in the biographies of men.... Here are lives I felt deserved exposure to more light."

In Part IV, she turns to quieter moments in the "biographies of men." Rather than celebrating their heroic deeds, she contemplates their domestic lives, imagining their inner monologues and journal entries: David's pause before slaying Goliath; Truman at the breakfast table before unleashing the A-bomb; Oppenheimer's regret.

Part V offers excerpts from *Hakugai*, a book-length narrative poem written in the voices of a Japanese-American family interned during World War II. Here she is concerned with the daily life of those whose courage in unjust circumstances has gone largely unrecognized.

Part VI consists of passages from *Heloise and Abelard: A Verse Play*, which was first produced by Edgar Lansbury at the Nicholas Roerich Theater in New York City in 1988. Again, she concerns herself with two figures struggling under the constraints of a forbidding society.

Part VII deals with writers who remained unrecognized during their lifetimes. She notes, "I am intrigued by those who find little or no worldly success or publication, and yet write on, and on and on, to the ends of their lives.... What forces keep some people writing? Fame, obviously, for some is *not* the spur. What, then, is?"

Finally, Part VIII gathers together those writings in which she contemplates loss, mourning, and the commemoration of the dead.

Geraldine Clinton Little was a writer who grappled with the most intimate of life's episodes—memories of childhood, death of loved ones, private delight in the natural world—as well as with more public concerns of social inequity and injustice. This volume is intended as a tribute to her enduring passion for life.

Amanda Field

A Little Bouquet

JOURNAL

Sometime I may have children. What will they think of me, whom they will know only as mother, never as child, girl, lover, teacher, the other things I am?

I keep this journal about you, Mama. One day I will give it to you and you may read how I see, saw, you, for I believe you are as curious as I about the multiple personalities we are. Eves, all of us, with many faces, fading from one to another like special effects no camera records.

This is sporadic, erratic, nothing disciplined about it, written at random when emotion dictates, or need.

Shame.

I am ashamed of you. It is summer and you are in your room looking out on the tree-brimmed street, reading, of course. I always think of you reading. It is just after supper and humid beyond bearing. I am 15. My God is "what others think." I look at you, damp and contented, lost in your other world. Why, why is there a dirty rim around the collar of your cotton dress? Having worked in it all day, why didn't you change it for dinner? Oh yes, I noticed it at dinner, the ten of us hungry as loosed hibernators.

I see the old, imperfect kitchen, the fey black oven that lights only upon incantation, with a great frightening pouf; see the icebox that is less than competent. More clearly, I see the gray depressed rim of the sweaty dress as I gobble your goodness. Why do you not look like the movie stars I see at the Saturday afternoon movie? Why, dinner done, have you still not changed?

I do not understand. I do not understand the old iron set up in your bedroom, the chair beside it piled with washed clothes. I am angry. You could, at least—my mind slips to the earlier irritation—wash.

It is early morning. You are playing the piano. You play splendidly, poignantly. Why not, your alma mater the London College of Music?

"But where is the blue skirt I must wear to school today?"

Your music breaks off. Apologetically, you run to that pile in your bedroom, unearth the skirt, and transform it to smooth. You bring it to me, in my slip combing my hair. It will not go in the right direction.

"How could you have forgotten it?" I scold.

"I'm sorry," you smile. "Shall I start your breakfast now?"

"In five minutes." I am distracted by a red something on my chin.

"You're so pretty, an anemone."

I frown. I barely hear you.

"That Irish family with all the dirty children."

I am going up the steps to my house after school. They think I cannot hear them, three popular Helens of our class. I want to cry; I want to kill them; I want to kill you.

Eight children. How could *anyone* have eight children? It is obscene. It is dirty, as we often are. Why are you so busy reading or playing the piano that you do not see that we are always clean, our clothes always immaculate?

When I go in, you are playing Bach. I hate Bach. I clatter down my books in the cluttered living room. Why haven't you cleaned it? Not a chair not piled with music or books, *Not a chair not piled with music or books*, I scream at you. Your music stops. I am glad I can stop your music, your reading. Why should you live in those worlds when we are in need?

You are in the garden. You are talking to plants, years before anyone heard of talking to plants. Your garden is eloquent, but your hands are dirty, so dirty. And where is the white blouse I *must* have for my date tonight? You drop spade and wash—both hands and blouse—and press it. I do not question that you wait on me. You are my mother; it is your *privilege*.

I am 22. We could not afford college for me. I work in an office. I feel like a misfit. These people have read nothing. I wander Hardy's country, or Little Gidding.

"You're a regular Cassandra," I shake my head at a coworker.

She looks at me, blankly. Should she be angry or glad? Have I insulted or praised?

I am bewildered. Where are people who have read anything? I see you reading to me each night, see myself picking up one of your books, dropped carelessly everywhere, see myself curled in its intricacies, from seven years to the present....

I am auditioning. I sing Bach. Well. I know it as I know my name. Yes, I am accepted for this prestigious chorus. I hear your endless Bach that I cut off for my endless necessities....

A date takes me to his home, a great estate with fine gardens.

"Lobelia," I exclaim, "lupine, oh the primroses."

"What queer things you know." He mixes a cocktail.

I want the tang of the garden, its wild ways....

I want to give you this journal, you with your love of the written word, of learning, however haphazardly persued. I take it to your room, in the middle of the night. This odd urgency.

You are not there. I knew that. I heard them carry you out this morning, the solemn feet of undertakers walking through snatched sleep. I am happy that you are not here, for you were in great pain for a long time.

I am happy that, when you could no longer see, I read you the journal, happy that we laughed and cried together over it, happy that I heard you angrily refute imprecise perceptions. I am happy I had the courage to share it with you, that I was able to show you sides of you that you might not have known, happy that I could thank you for great books and music and simple and splendid flowers.

I place it on your bedside table beside a glass of daisies.

Margaret, my mother.

I go to the window and look at the sky, starless and blank, blank as the blank white pages you will never read, that I have never written.

I am nude in my lie, in the make-believe I have almost believed.

The moon shows a silver, slim light, arriving too late.

from *Woman in a Special House*

LASTING RESONANCE

Listen, I can't help it. Sundays of my childhood
Father perched in the pulpit box, releasing
majestic, sonorous birds of language, the King
James version of miracles and mythologies, over my head
like a beautiful plague that struck me down forever.
How shall I learn to put away childish things,
to conjure the world in the innocent speech of the sparrow,
whose bones fleshed under the shadows of eagles?

from *A Well-Tuned Harp*

MISSES IN MEMORY

In quivering Irish mist you must have kissed
me goodbye. Did I smile, thinking
you'd be back when birds shut down the day,
would look in to see no covers smothered
a new baby's breath and forming limbs?

What is it about the first few years that won't
release memory? I can remember things from three:
a teaset with oddly mauve roses, tiny
knives and spoons, imaginary friends,
never those first few months. Did you hug me

before sailing to America for one year,
year I spent in other arms, not
a mother's? Why do I ask now, a woman
in mid-life with only happiest memories
of you, your music, your ardent love of flowers?

Because *loss* rattles in my bones, its own
skeleton trying to find form, or answer.
How could you leave me? It's like a DNA defect.
Unloved, not loved enough. I search the world
for the link: this bed, that bed, always lacking.

from *No Home to Return to But This*

THE DESERT SHALL REJOICE

Christmas and home are synonymous in my mind. Ours was a Christmas straight out of Dickens, a wonderful, sparkling event in our lives. In retrospect, it is our loveliest family remembrance. We look back on it as the perfect time; we who can never share it again. Though we may share Christmas now with our children, those Christmases, with Mama as their center, are in the shimmering wonderland of long-ago-and-never-again.

We were a very close family, my mother's sister (our beloved Ninny who had always lived with us), my three sisters and two brothers, all now married and away from home, my father and I, the youngest of the six children. We used to pity families with only one or two children. How *dead* those homes must be! Our household was a tremendous hive of bustling activity toward December 25th. Oh, the trimming, wrapping, cooking, writing, and receiving of cards, the playing of timeless Christmas music on the piano, Mama's expert fingers leading us all. Mama, a graduate of the London College of Music, had never let her music slip, six children and the active life of a minister's wife notwithstanding.

Buying for Christmas, 1949, had been such fun! Mama and I had gone shopping, gayly, through crowds and dancing snow. With what delight we found a record of "The Teddybears' Picnic," first popular that year and a perfect gift for several of Mama's 14 grandchildren. Eight of the 14 grandchildren were with us that year, in addition to the nine of us, plus my sisters' and brothers' respective spouses. As for so many years before, Mama and Dada unobtrusively directed activities, and we were children still. After dinner music rang through the house, Mama at the piano, Dada playing the violin, and we singing in parts, as we had been trained to do as tots.

The only shadow cast on the festivities was that Mama had a very slight, ever-present earache, but she rarely spoke of it and never let it stop her enjoyment. We, callous as people often are about someone else's slight sickness, paid as little attention to it as she apparently did.

Too soon that wonderful Yuletide was over, and the family members again took up their separate lives in widely scattered cities, leaving Mama, Ninny, and me to carry on with the dull routine of January, always a "let-down" month. Dada, a Home Missionary for the Board of Home Missions in New York, went off on a month's trip through Indiana.

The earache which had bothered Mama through the holiday season, still, in the middle of January, remained. Our friendly general practitioner, who had given Mama several treatments for an ear infection, told us one day, quite casually, that since the earache was still there, he'd like Mama to see a specialist. So, cheerily, she went off to Dr. Williams, laughing aside my suggestion that I accompany her. At dinner that evening she told us, in her calm way, that her earache was slightly worse, because Dr. Williams had taken a small piece from inside the ear to put through analysis.

"Just routine, he says," she told us, and Ninny and I, ignorant of the medical world and its workings (for we were singularly free of illness in our family), accepted the statement and tucked Mama into bed at an early hour, a heating pad on the offending ear.

At work the next day my brother phoned me and told me that Dr. Williams had called him and advised him that Mama had a serious mastoidal condition and must have an operation at once. Dr. Williams, Trevor told me, was making immediate arrangements for Mama's entrance into hospital. They would operate two days later, at 2 p.m. I put down the receiver, only half believing. It had been so abrupt a statement; I had been so totally unprepared for it. Mama seriously ill? Mama, who in her small person embodied immeasurable moral strength for us all, and indeed physical strength as well. One of my mental pictures of her is the sight of her effortlessly moving her beloved piano around the drawing room, alone. Surely my brother was mistaken, had somehow misunderstood Dr. Williams.

But it was, after all, terribly true. That evening we drove Mama to the hospital. All of us, particularly Mama herself, made brave remarks about how fine it would be when this was all over and she would be home, quite well, planting, with her usual joy and enthusiasm, her spring garden. Why, mastoids are nothing these days, we all assured one another, fear lying like some gray ghost on our hearts as, inevitably, Ninny and I had to leave her, looking so game and cheery, and so small and defenseless in the stark hospital bed.

Dada arrived home the next morning, having been summoned by Trevor. After 40 years together they were not to be separated in this crisis. Dada, true to character, covered up his terrible fear and bewilderment with his usual blustering, histrionic manner. But Mama was glad to have him home. Of course, she didn't say as much. They were of the outwardly undemonstrative Victorian era, but their very casualness and brusqueness told you they were lovers still.

Having installed a television set in Mama's room, to which she consented, I am sure, more to please us than because she wanted it, we had to leave. There were many preparations to be made by the hospital staff for the next day's operation.

I went to work the following day. There are times when work is the most wonderful thing in the world. I gratefully cleaned out files and brought up to date certain records—jobs I had been putting off for weeks. At 2 p.m. my mind flew to the hospital. The thought of my kind, gentle, loving mother going under the surgeon's knife was a nightmare to me. It seemed an unutterably lonely experience. We who loved her so much could not be with her, could not help her. She was among stark-white strangers. I tried to continue working at the furious pace I had set myself that morning, but I could not keep my mind off the scene centered around an operating table, where my mother, my dear Mama, was, for once in her shy, retiring life, the center of attention.

I phoned home several times during the next two hours, but there was no word. Mama was still in the operating room. When I arrived home at 5 p.m., I learned that Mama had only just come out of the operating room, at 4:30. Two-and-one-half hours! It was apparently a more complicated operation than any of us had suspected.

The next morning we went to see Mama. (We had not been allowed to come the night before). The gallant little figure, head swathed in bandages, brought tears to our eyes. But she was as calm, kind, optimistic, and interested as always. She wanted to know all that had been happening. Had we played canasta last night? Had Dada rested enough after his trip? Was my cold better? No thought for herself, but only for us. This was the essence of Mama.

She seemed so well. We called Dr. Williams and thanked him for performing such a fine operation for us, and, if his reply was guarded, we did not notice in the excitement of knowing that Mama was all right and was coming home to us.

In only two days she *was* home, head still almost completely covered with bandages, but what matter. She was home! Our strangely silent, waiting house became alive again.

It was a week later, at luncheon on Saturday, that I noticed that one side of Mama's mouth had dropped, giving her face a twisted, crooked look. I mentioned it to Ninny later, and she said, yes, she had noticed but had said, of course, nothing to Mama. Dada was too wrapped up in his job of "getting Mama better," which consisted largely of forcing her to eat things she did not want, but which she gamely struggled to down, a daily ritual which irritated me beyond measure, to notice the sadly drooping mouth. Ninny and I discussed it and decided that probably with the healing of the wound the mouth would come back into proper shape. Nevertheless, we made note to ask Dr. Williams about it on Mama's next visit to him.

I went about my daily executive-secretary job with a lighter heart than I had had in weeks. Mama's convalescence seemed slow, but it was of no moment as long as she was home with us and we could care for her and could, unconsciously, draw our strength from her. Mastoidal operation patients, Dr. Williams had told us, always made a slow recovery. This we, in turn, told Mama when she, rarely and hesitatingly, as if she were afraid of bothering us, asked if we thought she was making any progress.

So I was very surprised one day when my brother, Trevor, came on a rare visit to my office and said he would like to talk to me about Mama. Of course, I said, offering him a chair, What was there to talk about, I wondered? Trevor went right to the point. Dr. Williams had called Trevor to his office and had told him the entire facts of Mama's case. She had cancer of the ear. He had had to remove the ear, and, when he operated, he found the cancer had already spread too far. Mama had about six months to live.

I have no recollection of Trevor's leaving. I do not remember working that afternoon. I do vividly remember a series of flashbacks which my mind presented. Whether it was for a moment or an hour, I don't know. But I spent in retrospect what seemed like days. A hundred pictures of Mama came to mind. Mama teaching me early piano essentials; Mama joyously playing hymns on Sunday morning— our first sound on that day; Mama buying me a pair of gay red pajamas one Christmas, because I especially wanted them; Mama ceaselessly reading books by herself and to us. Knowing my love of our cat, Mama waking me in the morning with a cheery, "The cat's back, ducky!" after one of kitty's three-or-four-day jaunts; Mama, possessor of the original emerald thumb, happily taking a slip of some plant she particularly wanted, from the arboretum.

"Of course it's not stealing," she would indignantly insist when one of us pointed out that this practice probably was frowned upon in the best arboretum circles. "Plants and trees belong to God." And my dear Mama, scrupulously honest in every detail, could never be brought to see that some officials really are stuffy about this sort of thing! Mama, who stayed on at the failing downtown church as organist long years after my father had left it as pastor, trailing down to it, an hour's journey each way by streetcar on Sunday morning, often wheezing with the asthma that sometimes plagued her in winter. In vain did we plead with her to give it up, uselessly we pointed out that for the four or five old people still attending, some neighborhood pianist would do. Our insistence that she at least not give back in the collection the entire small salary they still paid her fell on deaf ears. "They need it; it's my duty," said Mama, and that was that! Duty to Mama was as the Rock of Gibraltar. Nothing we could say to this gentlest of women could budge her.

Mama's music was the theme that ran through all my reminiscences. She could read any piece of music, play anything by ear, and transpose anything into any key. As I made an effort to start to type that terrible afternoon, I could see Mama gayly and beautifully playing the old, lovely Irish airs she knew so well and loved. I heard her playing Chopin's "Fantasie Impromptu" so beautifully one almost could not bear it. I used to think that in her music she went back again to her girlhood days in Ireland—carefree, golden days when she had been, as my grandmother had often told us, "the belle of the county." Mama's later life had not been easy, though it had been, essentially, happy. Used to the best of everything, and to being "county," it had, I was sure, been hard for her to become used to the rigid life of a minister's wife, with six small mouths to feed on a less-than-slim budget. And so I felt that music was her release, that in its mystical realm she lost herself and dreamed dreams of the green island she loved and was never able to revisit. That she had, now, lost her ear seemed the cruelest of fates.

The day of my brother's visit ended, unbelievably, and I went home to dinner not knowing how I could face Mama, how I could keep her from seeing the anguish that filled my heart and mind. But something or someone gives us strength. I remember with crystal clarity that I told a number of gay stories at dinner, even one which made Mama laugh. A few moments later I could have cut my throat gladly, for apparently that small excitement was more than Mama could stand. She had to throw up, there at the dinner table. She apologized abjectly to us for upsetting our dinner, thinking of us again, not of herself and the terrible pain that bout of illness caused her. I left the table and went to my room where, lacking Mama's great courage, I lay on my bed and cried, and cried.... At length I slid to my knees and prayed an unbelievable prayer that God would take Mama from us soon and end her hideous, unaidable suffering. Bitterly, I felt that was the least He could do.

Incurable cancer follows a pattern, as anyone who has had it in their family knows. The patient is given dope to alleviate pain, and progressively more dope as an immunity to the earlier amount builds up. Dr. Williams started Mama with large white pills. Today I can sketch their size accurately. We gave Mama so many, so frequently.

When each one was just about wearing off, Mama's pain, ever constant but dulled by the pill, would start to come to the fore before the next pill we had given her took effect.

One of us, every other day, drove Mama the three miles to Dr. Williams's office where he re-bandaged the wound. Mama and Dr. Williams became fast friends. Mama was so gallant and so radiantly good, so uncomplaining in the face of what must have been almost unbearable pain. Dr. Williams had in his waiting room all manner of beautifully blooming plants, some very rare. Through all her agony, Mama's lifelong love of anything growing asserted itself, and she and Dr. Williams exchanged slips and plant lore along with bandages.

Those trips to Dr. Williams's office, however, were nightmares. Every bump, though slight, was as a searing knife in Mama's head. We crawled down the busy thoroughfares so as not to jar her, but this gave impatient, unknowing drivers an opportunity to lie on their horns. Their blasts echoed through poor Mama's head; it was heartrending to see her in agony and be helpless in the face of it. Upon arrival at Dr. Williams's office she was done in and would have to have a hypodermic needle before he could work on her. Shortly, the insistent, jabbing, relentless pain would settle to a dull ache, and she would be interestingly chatting with her friend and doctor about his plants.

After the large white pills came very small white ones, but soon these were of no value taken orally. She was then put upon hypodermic needles full time. At first, having had some experience with giving herself needles for asthma, she took this chore upon herself. The day soon came when she was too weak to do this, and I took over the job. I can never describe, and I will never forget, what it cost me to jab poor Mama's leg or arm, each already dotted with angry red specks from the hated, yet wonderful, needle.

But what it cost me was as nothing to what Mama was going through. Just before the needle Ninny or I would often come on her, head in hands, crying softly to herself, "Oh, what shall I do, what shall I do." Then, as she saw us, she would become very quiet and would patiently wait until I had given her the blessed needle. How many times in the night Ninny or I arose to prepare and administer the hypodermic, for Ninny, too, soon learned how to give it. The procedure was to dissolve one little white pill in a teaspoon of water over a small old oil lamp we had rigged up outside Mama's door, Then carefully, very carefully, so that no air got in, we sucked this solution up into the needle. I cannot begin to say what Ninny was to Mama during that terrible six months. Her labor was a labor of love indeed. She quite literally wore herself out in caring tenderly, lovingly, unceasingly, for my mother. She was with Mama all day and often all night. No task was too menial nor too great, if it would help Mama. She was her sister's keeper.

But everyone was good to Mama. It was easy to be; she had spent her life being kind and good to us. How little it was, really, for my married sisters to arrange their own homes and lives so that they could come and spend a few days, alternately, with us, helping to take care of Mama.

I wonder if, during their moments with her, they have any remembrances as bitter and unerasable as mine? There was the Sunday morning when I was alone with Mama. Ninny had gone to church, one of the rare occasions when she consented to leave her post of love and duty, and none of my sisters was then visiting us. Mama's poor mouth was terribly dry, yet a drink of water always made her nauseous. She took her false teeth out and asked me to run cold water over them and bring them back. I am a stupidly fastidious creature about such things. I hate to touch other people's false teeth; I hate the sight of blood; I loathe cleaning up after someone has been ill. In short, it is small wonder that nursing has not been my chosen profession. When Mama handed out her teeth, I hesitated, infinitesimally, but long enough for my dear, sensitive mother to know what was going through my mind. But there was no anger, no resentment. "Poor ducky" was all she said. "I know how you hate it, but it would be such a relief." I can never forget that Sunday, nor should I be allowed to.

There was the evening my father was hovering over Mama, forcing her to eat something she did not want and had already refused. Trying, as usual, to please, Mama finally consented to take a spoonful, although she knew full well, and we knew, that it would immediately make her sick. That particular night it was more than I could stand. I screamed at him to let her alone. He, a highly sensitive man, with a keen but wholly unstudied instinct for the dramatic, looked amazed for an instant, then went into the dining room, put his head down on his hands and cried with sobs that seemed to tear his heart out, in between making statements to the effect that I was crucifying him.

I wanted to run wildly out into the night. To think that, in trying to help Mama, I had created this terrible scene while she was dying—*was dying!*—was more than I could bear. True to character, Mama herself was the peacemaker, soothing Dada and saying just the right things to me, and never mentioning the fact that her pain was becoming unbearable and that needle-time was imminent.

One never forgets these things; they remain our crosses, our burdens to bear, in silence and alone.

Often, during those terrible months, we read to Mama her favorite chapter from the Bible, the 35th chapter of Isaiah. My mother was a deeply religious woman, although not volubly. Her religion was as simple as a child's. She believed in, and lived by, the principles of Christianity, with no fuss or strain, and with a good Irish sense of humor. Her religion was not a matter of conjecture or theological debate. She *knew* that "sorrow and sighing shall flee away." We who loved her so much tried to comfort her in her solitary world of pain, but what could we offer that was worth even half what she found in the Book that had sustained her for some 60 years? When her eyes failed so that she could no longer read at all (Mama—the omnivorous reader!), we used to find, after a hypodermic had put her to sleep oh so temporarily, the Bible closed on her finger, marking this chapter of Isaiah.

It was about five months after Mama first became ill that we had to tell her that Dr. Williams had died, suddenly, of a heart attack. She said little, only instructed us to send his favorite flowers, one of the plants they had discussed with such enthusiasm. Then she seemed to retire a little farther into herself, and the great reservoirs of courage and understanding that were hers. Did she, in her deep wisdom, know that she would soon be joining him; that the parting from this good kind friend was temporary; that they would meet again in a land covered with blossoms such as they had never known on earth?

For we had never told Mama that her time with us was limited. We had avoided all mention of her true illness and had been careful to tell her that the needles she was taking were to make her better, but that this was a long, arduous illness, slow to cure. This was the climate of silence about cancer of that time. In my mind now I am sure we underestimated Mama. She had always been an unusually intelligent woman. I don't think we ever fooled her. I think she knew, and, thinking to save us any awkwardness or embarrassment or pain in having to speak of death, let us think she thought she was getting better. But gradually she prepared herself for what was to come next, and, I think, tried to prepare us. She prayed often, quietly, sincerely, simply, and with great dignity.

Some of us became daily more bitter toward God. Why had He singled out our mother, a saint indeed, whose whole life had been spent in His service, for this terrible, unabated form of torture? But Mama never seemed to question, never blamed. It was as if she knew, somehow, the purpose of it all.

"Oh, Lord, help me to stand it," was all I ever heard her say, and that, in moments of deepest agony, with tears running down her face, so that I wanted to take her in my arms and comfort her, as she had so often comforted me.

Mama was rapidly becoming weaker. One day she climbed into bed, never to leave it again in this life. "Let me die in peace," she wrote on the back of an old envelope, almost illegibly, for she now could not see at all and could barely speak, the effort was so great.

The whole family came then, my three sisters and two brothers, to join Ninny, Dada, and myself in constant vigil as we waited, dry-eyed, tear-drenched inside, for Mama to leave us. We took turns remaining by her bedside so that she would never be alone for a moment. It was so terribly, unspeakably lonely, this journey she had to take. We loved her so much; she was so dear to us, the motivating force in our close family circle, but in the end we could do nothing for her.

While I was by her side, she woke, once, out of her state of final coma and cried, pitifully, weakly, "Who is there?" I told her and she whispered, "Oh, Gerrie, my baby, you know I love you." And she held me for a moment so strongly, for the last time in her arms, then dropped back into unconsciousness, while I, tears streaming down my face, gave her, following doctor's instructions, one last hypodermic in her legs, already cold and no longer Mama,

It was just toward dawn on July 1, 1950, that Dada called us into Mama's room. We saw Mama pass peacefully and as gently as she had done everything all her life, from her world of agony into a world where "the eyes of the Blind shall be opened, and the ears of the deaf shall be unstopped. The parched ground shall become pools and the thirsty land springs of water."

And the day broke, and the shadows flew away.

Unpublished

SLIPPAGE

Father, Mother, you embraced
Weil, her transcendent goodness. I try
to sit on the sky, to see

what you saw, secure in the Cross
and bloodied Lamb, but I fall
again and again into the wilderness

of brain cells and synapses
that tell me God
may be a woman used to crosses,

the monthly blood shed,
the white wings
of clothes repetitively strung,

may be the silken wing
of a bee at a rose,
the rose itself anointed with rain,

the globe of an apple
hanging against the moon,
the moon advancing, retreating,

may be light from a star
born before Christ clutched it,
is never the Father

hands full of cancer and poverty
of flesh and spirit pacing
the world's four winds.

I whisper denial,
deny the high throne of His sky
but affirm my place

on earth, its muddy stench,
its rutting masses, those mysteries
sufficient for a lifetime's labor.

Yet I wonder, Simone, Mother,
Father, how did you manage
the cosmic leap

I long for when I am sucked,
sometimes, into the black hole
beyond cells and senses?

    from *A Well-Tuned Harp*

A Summer Afternoon

"*I* would have preferred scones," the Reverend Alexander Moore stated with authority to his wife, who had just handed him a thick slice of Irish soda bread heaped with gooseberry jam.

"They're no good cold, Alex, you know that. The bread's fresh. Made just before we left." Margaret Moore, a shy, brown wren of a woman, was almost apologetic. "It's your favorite jam," she added hopefully.

"Mm—and very good it is, too."

Margaret's held breath began again. She had so been afraid of an explosion of temperament, of which the reverend was brim full.

"I do love a picnic, an afternoon in the open air. There's nothing like it." Alex stretched the six feet two inches of him on a spread car blanket over which Margaret, his Meg, had laid a white cloth and mounds of picnic fare. Leaning on one elbow, Alex held a cup of strong tea—"I like the spoon to almost stand tip in it, Meg, you know that."—in one hand, the slab of bread on a plate before him. His almost black eyes looked out over the creek where they often came in summer, Alex, Meg, and their two daughters, for a picnic and a swim. It was free, a consideration that was constant in the lives of the Moores.

"It's lovely, dear." Meg busied herself with unpacking the home-grown tomatoes her husband loved. Where was the salt? Hard-boiled eggs. Homemade lemon tarts. Meg always had to get the provender together in short order.

After a morning of visitation on a fine summer day, Alex would come home on the upswing end of his mood cycle and call, "Moira, Ethna. What about going to the creek for a picnic? Meg? Is there any food?"

And of course there was, for Meg baked fresh soda bread daily, as her mother had done all Meg's growing years in Portstewart on the northern coast of Ireland.

Tomatoes sang on the vine, mouth-ready. They were Alex's "gardening." He was stentorian proud of the few vines that gave them fresh red rounds throughout the summer. When guests came to

Sunday tea, a custom kept from European days, Alex shamelessly extolled his prowess with tomatoes. "Love apples, you know. More tea, Miss Greenwood?"

Meg cared for the rest of the garden, quietly.

While the others were gathering fishing equipment—"Where is my tackle box, Meg?" "In the shed by the washer, dear." Where you left it, Meg never said aloud—Meg made delectable lemon tarts in minutes, and hard-boiled eggs. The girls piled into a large hamper silverware, china plates, and cups. Alex could not abide paperware. "Poor weak instruments, a curse of the devil, soggy and tinting everything with the taste of cardboard." So Meg brought linen napkins from her mother's chest, a nostalgic legacy, pristine and crisp in silver napkin rings three generations old.

Moira slipped a napkin ("Mama called them serviettes, Moira," Meg had once mused) from her ring, slapdash wiped her month, and said to Ethna, "What about a walk through the trees?" At twelve, Moira had learned to say nothing before her father that was not bland, nothing that could be taken issue with. Which was quite brilliant of her, given Alexander Moore's lawyer-like techniques on any, on every, question or statement.

Ethna, ten, not yet so sophisticated in the way of "handling Father," was about to say, "But I'd rather walk to the rope swing." Moira quickly said, "Come, I'll make you a clover chain. You'll be Miriam-who-watched Moses, and I'll be one of the serving women."

Ethna rose to this with delight. "Oh, I'd *love* to be Miriam." She swallowed the last of her tangy tart and followed her sister. "Will you make me a bracelet, too, Moira?"

"Yes, and ankle bracelets if you want them." Moira tried to keep impatience from her voice. *Let's get away from them. Let's go where we can breathe.*

"That's mildly blasphemous, Moira. I doubt that Miriam wore such baubles," Alexander looked up from his job of inspecting fishhooks.

"Of course, you are right, Dada," Moira said, "but since they're flowers of the field, I think God won't mind."

Moira would go far.

"Mm, I suppose not. Be careful, then. Ach, my reel's stuck." He shook the offending reel. Under cover of that distraction, Moira and Ethna left the stretch of cleared bank where they were picnicking and slipped into the wood that bordered the creek.

This was what they loved, this bower they felt was their own. Oaks, older than anyone could imagine, lay on a wonderfully blue sky. Had it really always been so blue? Moira was to wonder in after years. There were never clouds. Birds somersaulted and cartwheeled through the trees and tangled vines, the while singing, a feat the girls thought miraculous. Which it was.

They wore nothing but bathing suits. Everyone put on bathing suits at home before leaving, and slipped easy clothes over the suits for quick doffing when they arrived at the picnic site. A paper bag held underwear for going home.

They all loved the water. Dada was a great swimmer, had won races in his youth round the cold headland waters of Ireland. Meg "bathed." She had never learned to swim, a defect of character Alex tried always to correct.

"Just come as far as my hand," he'd say, going out beyond the small rock-enclosed shallow area where Meg felt safe. But she could not, the only thing she would not do for her husband, her only mild disobedience. She dipped up and down, happy in safe water.

Disgusted, Dada, in earlier years, turned to the girls. His method of getting them to swim was to carry them to the top of the "diving" rock and simply toss them into deep water.

"It's a natural instinct, girls," he had said before the first toss. "No one teaches dogs to swim; they simply do. So will you."

"Mama doesn't," Ethna pointed out before she had learned better.

That brought down a ten-minute sermon and made Mama so miserable that Ethna wanted to cry. Only Moira's hand strongly squeezing hers kept her from making things worse, which would have meant another sermon.

So they were thrown in.

"Wasn't it terrible, terrible, Moira?" Ethna whispered to her sister later when they were alone. "The whole creek in my mouth, the weeds...."

"It was terrible," Moira said in her determined way. "And unforgivable of Dada. We could have drowned, as indeed I thought I was going to. The awful choking, the gasping at nothing, the current dragging me on."

Ethna *did* cry then. The tears of relief, tears of rage. Tears of desperation.

But they learned to swim. Well. Strongly. It left Moira with ambivalent, half-frightened feelings about Alexander Moore's God that they did not develop impossible trauma from the experience. For they did not. Both were to swim, loving it, to the end of their lives. Moira felt, finally that it had more to do with Dada's will than God's.

Now twigs and vines brushed their tanned skin as they wound through the trail they knew led to, of course, the bank where the rope swing hung over a sun-touched stretch of the creek.

"You must never tell Dada that we come here," Moira chastised her sister as they looked at the knotted end swaying slightly in an infinitesimal breeze.

"Why not, he loves us to swim?" Ethna's eyes, like the color of blown grasses, widened.

"He does *not* like us to swing on the rope. Don't you remember how he raged after he saved that boy on the far creek last year? No, I forgot. You weren't there."

"I was sick." Ethna remembered the fevered dreams, the sweated sheets.

"Well. The boy and his family picnicked near us. The rope swing hung nearby. He shinnied up it and worked himself into a fine motion. He dropped off into a rock half in the water. He was out cold," Moira related with delight.

"Oh Moira, did he die?"

"No. He slid away under the water, and Dada rescued him, gave him mouth-to-mouth, which was *quite* horrid, and the boy gasped like a fish and was all right. Wasn't he stupid to drop on a rock?"

"Surely he didn't mean to, Moira." Ethna scanned the water under their rope swing. There were some rocks at the shoreline.

"Of course not, silly, but he ought to have taken more care." Moira would have been appalled had anyone told her she sounded rather like her father. "So Dada said that day that we were never ever to go on a rope swing." Moira stared at the long twisted thing someone—who?—had attached to a limb of oak.

"Then why—why do we?" Ethna ventured.

Moira turned to her young sister. "Because, my dear, we are *not* silly or careless, and because—it's marvelous fun!" Moira raced to the rope and began to shinny up it.

She did this more easily than Ethna, but still it wasn't easy. The hemp was tough. It was like nettles pricking her. Sometimes she slipped a bit. Her hands reddened, ripped. Once, the rope had rubbed the patch between her legs. The sensation that overtook her was ecstasy; the little clitoris throbbed, throbbed. Moira had almost fallen. That had never occurred again, however much she tried to recapture, to duplicate the maneuvers that led to it.

At last she reached the top. She could stretch out, if she dared loose one hand from the rope, and touch the oak limb holding the rope.

Moira stared down, down at the muddied mirror beneath her. It held everything; it held the world. Look, a bird drifted into a stand of pines. There was another rope, rippled and shadowy. There was a girl on the rope and where would she fall to? Into the sky that was always blue?

Moira called to her sister, who pulled the rope back toward

shore and suddenly let it go.

"How would you like to go up in a swing?" Moira sang to a curious crow.

Back, forth.

Then she let go. Oh, there was nothing like it. She was a bird. Or a butterfly. She existed only in air. She was free of her body, her bones, her burden of sermons and don'ts and God.

The cold creek water opened its arms to her. The shock was a kaleidoscope of delight, like a wanted explosion in her head. Mauve, greens never seen before, a burst of pinky-beige, a shout of blue.

She opened her eyes in the muddy depths. She had not touched bottom but a world of weeds that kissed her legs eerily. There were bubbles. *Why* were there bubbles? The bubbles were magical balls of rainbow. Her hair plumed, danced around her, lashing her face, wandering away as if in wind. She was light, light. All ways were light.

Moira popped through the creek's skin, gasping, laughing. She waved to Ethna, whose hand was at her mouth shaped like an O. Moira floated a moment, to catch her breath. She watched the sky with its furniture of trees, birds. If God lived in that splendid house, why did He thunder so? Why wasn't He happier?

"Moira, come on, swing me," Ethna called. Moira sighed, swam to shore, picked her way through pebbles and mud at the edge.

"It's wonderful, wonderful, Ethna. It's the world. Here. I'll hold the rope steady while you go."

Up the rope, fall away to the kingdom of water and sky in that water, breath leaping, the heart dancing. Over and over again. Until they were exhausted.

They lay on a patch of weedy grass, silent, filled.

"I'll make you a crown," Moira said suddenly, out of the silence. "And bracelets."

"Yes, you'd better, or Dada will ask questions."

"We could tell him we threw them away."

"We could, but that would be a lie, Moira."

Moira looked at her young sister. "Yes, so it would." She began to fashion jewels of clover, making a hole in the stem of one, carefully, carefully, so it didn't rip. As carefully, she pulled the stem of another clover through the little hole, until the flowerhead stopped its passage.

"Would you like to have been Miriam?" Ethna asked when, gemmed, she stood by a birch, touching her crown.

Moira considered. "No, I'd rather be the Egyptian princess. But, Ethna, suppose Miriam hadn't watched Moses. Suppose there had been a rope swing strung up near the bulrushes and she climbed up it and fell away into another world. Suppose *that*, Ethna. Where would Moses be?"

Ethna thought. "In Egypt, wouldn't he?"

"No," said Miriam. "He would not. He would have drifted away on the stream, away, away to the ocean. Why, he might have drifted to *Ireland*, Ethna, and lived with kings of Ireland. You're Ethna/Miriam, Princess of Ireland." Moira laughed, scooped water from the creek and put it on her sister's head. "There, I've christened you, Princess Ethna."

"Oh, Moira," Ethna laughed, too. The birches and oaks trembled with laughter. The rocks clapped their hands and the green weedy earth chuckled.

"What about God?" Ethna asked, suddenly.

"What *about* God?" Moira frowned.

"He wouldn't have allowed that, you know. Why you've changed the *Bible*, Moira."

"So I have." Moira scribbled in the dirt with a stick.

Ethna shivered. "We must go back, Moira, the sun's going down. Dada will be furious with us." She tore off the crown, the wrist and ankle bracelets as if they burned her. "Come on, Moira, come *on*."

Moira lingered at the creek edge for a moment. She looked up at the rope just barely swaying. She looked at the water beneath and the sky above.

"It's the time in the air that's the best," she said aloud. "After you let go of the rope, before you enter the water, *that's* the best time."

Moira turned and went after her sister through the wood.

She noticed a few leaves turning blood red. Autumn was near, and, after it, winter. She saw the rope hanging, snow-whitened over iced water.

But the air would be there, waiting.

Yes.

She gathered up the innocence of her summer face, an offering to her father.

from *Woman in a Special House*

TREASURER OF MY FATHER'S CHURCH

He was the man, plump as a blown-up balloon,
pompous in tailor-made suits
(stuffs from England, he'd work
like necessary threads
into any conversation, hands
hooked like medals
into popping seams of his waistcoats),
who practiced juggling
coins and important paper
in the building downtown
I thought dour as a rainy day without books;
gray, endless, nothing like
the Victorian grandeur of his home
(all bows and candles, wreath-looped lamps,
paisley cloths on numerous tables
cluttered with glittering framed people
unreal to me as miles of rooms fraught
with ponderous furniture)
we were summoned to for dutiful dinners,
servants at crisp-aproned attention,
carving knives flourished
like dueling swords
above roasts and silver-dished vegetables.

Such expertise
could be banked on
in Depression days
to float the church
like an ark
through flooding waters
to solvency's Ararat.

Just once
I heard my father cry.
Hidden behind the half-open door
of his study, I heard his voice

break, like a corner of stained glass
hit at just the right angle to shatter
the whole, on the words

why must I beg again for my check
again overdue a week?

What does a child know,
youngest of six all at home?

Father, I never have found
any dove returned,
any olive branch
that could cover
the slivered wounds
of such nakedness.

from *A Well-Tuned Harp*

Singing the Dream

In a small shop in Ireland, my grandfather
is tapping nails into a shoe, his honorable trade.
Gulls clatter along the coastline.
In her cluttered parlor my grandmother
is playing hymns on the pump organ.
This is a long time ago
I have walked into out of the din
of America.
                          I pull up a chair
beside my grandmother. I begin to sing.
She doesn't hear me, for *she* is singing
to my mother sweet in her womb, she
who will move among daisies and primroses,
a young girl with no thought
that I am waiting for her
to hold me, as she dies,
a long shuddering moment, before she returns
to my grandmother's otherworldly music
I am listening to in the salt-touched air
of a green place, my grandfather setting the meter
for dreaming.

Now Granny moves
from Godsongs to the brown teapot,
pours out the substance
of our lives.
          from *A Well-Tuned Harp*

Contrasts in Keening

1

Portstewart, Ireland. Born here. Burst into air
spray nuzzled, mist licked, sea lapped. Selective, sun
came and comes, rare guest over the fair
hills, the tipsy gait of the sea's run.
Overlooking littered sand a curve of cobbles
promenades brisk with mongers: fish, green-
grocer, butcher, draper, tourist's baubles
(shamrocks, bog oak), a tobacconist's demesne.
Up a narrow stone staircase open
to elements another level of the town
meanders, finally twists away to a glen.
On this level wind-slapped houses sit down
simply to stare at the walled harbor's austere
outlines, fishing-boat brimmed when I lived here,

2

I hear, with no remembrance of it. Two
years was all my time on a great rock
on the higher level: a manse, ministerial frock
of my father's calling shaping direction. The new,
sinuous, lured him, always. The long view
from home led over the sea's list and knock
away from circumscribed lines, the liquid lock
of the sea, limited work and retinue,
however pleasant. He was forty, time
men wander. Ever original, he took
not off alone, banal middle-aged crime,
but wife, six children, mother-in-law, shook
sod and sand away in summertime
and sailed for the new world, no backward look

3

he said, but sang old songs in a new land,
spelled ancient tales, customs, kept alive
before my maturing eyes the stretch of strand
silvered in his telling. He would contrive
to tell us how tea tasted not like tea
but like some god-brewed glory, *only* in
that island scrimmed by mist, ardently
awash with words, music's poignant din.
Regret was not his portion or his bent.
He throve on scope of opportunity
that was "The States," but when has ever been rent
from an Irishman's roots his memory
of bog and bough, leprechaun in gorse
and greener ground than any grown? Of course

4

I had to go there, slip my hand inside
divinity that formed the faceted base
of sermons, creativity, his sure grace.
At twenty-two, alone, shy, pride
cloistering chattering fright at the long ride
(my first) in a frail plane across sea space,
I flew to find the unremembered place
where I was born, remote family for guide.
"You must see Cousin Hazel in the Wicklow
hills, she'll treat you royally, and oh
the purple of the hills. Pick up a stick
of blackest thorn and wander them. Go
to Belfast in the North. You'll have your pick
of relatives to put you up. No

5

one close now in Portstewart, but it's no drive
from Belfast. They'll take you there, wind
along the Coast Road, picnic by the live
lashing sea, wild primrose intertwined
with rock and whin." Their voices cracked, they shooed
me on the plane, not seeing. I watched earth fall
away within their waves, warmed by the brood
I had of letters to a random sprawl
of relatives. I gathered up a book
(my old retreat), but saw no words. Home
hovered on the page but had the look
of green and faery, gulls and tilting foam.
...Then Shannon shone out of my unsought sleep
and I was home, bones knocking... "It's a bit steep,"

6

my cousin said, we slipping through the hills
in a Hillman to her home set in a wood
I thought, approaching, beyond all woods. Could
anything be as lovelier, statelier? Rills
sang through violets, golden spills
of flowers. A splendid drive wound to where stood
in gray stone dignity that had withstood
long time, the manor, frilled with daffodils.
There was more manner in the laden tea
set handsomely before a prancing fire
in the patrician drawing room. See-through
thin Doulton, and Father was no liar.
Tea here *was* glory. Familiarity
flamed to the marrow: home. "You may acquire

7

a taste for it." I stared. Did she interpret
silence as distaste? Dear dirty Dublin
she'd driven me to; Georgian, gracious. Eyes met,
were conquered utterly by sprawling spin
of buildings, places known by book and tale
we drove near. I made proper noises, then
her stiff austerity walled off the gale
buffeting my belly. Gracious, when
I mentioned "Meeting of the Waters," Kil-
larney (youth is trite), she gave grave smile
and Hillmanned everywhere above the spill
of my romanticism, my held-back style
crumbling, wildflowers flaring forth. I think
lips cracked a bit when I trained North.... "Our link

8

is through third cousins," the man was beaming, tall
and red-mustached (quite like the snaps exchanged
for easy meeting), who crunched my hand, arranged
affairs with Customs, booted bags in Vauxhall,
and veered through Belfast traffic to a small
suburb, with warm efficiency. Ranged
down villa steps, expressions open, changed
from chaste good manners lately left, a tall
big-bosomed woman and three children met
and welcomed me with hearty, friendly ease.
"The kettle's on the boil, the table's laid.
You must be starved. A wash and then..." The breeze
of her enfolded me like arms. She made
me one of them, at once. "We can all squeeze

9

in Norman's car, the picnic basket in
the boot." A moist sun mauved next morning after
a sleep like cozy death, breakfast, sin-like
in scope, of eggs and tea. Laughter,
goodwill brimmed the car. We headed toward
Portstewart. "I wonder, is the duckpond there?
They used to swim in it." One of a horde
of tales my family told. It wasn't fair,
I'd thought, left out, the scenes they shared not mine.
"Still there and little changed. You'll see." I saw
the gray road edged with gorse twist up, incline
at last to the layered town below. Bones raw
to birthplace emanations, I stepped from the car
to stare down levels tumbling to sea. "Are

10

you aware we've parked by the manse and church? The
time I spent here…" Norman pointed right. Gray
against the clouds, structures stood the stolid way
they assumed the page in family albums. "Climb
up. The manse is locked—vacation. Daytime,
the church is open." The old door creaked. May
fell away to other time, play
of light on pulpit caught my father's clime.
I knew this place. Norman led my eyes,
clogged pools, down slim stone steps to promenade,
the harbor, fishing boats, the fall and rise
of gulls, spray singing off sea walls. It had
looked almost so since Viking era. Likewise
the nearby duckpond, now cemented. "Sad?"

11

Norman touched my shoulder. "No." How
explain emotion's mix? No need. He saw
and spoke no more as thrust waves thrashed. "Now,
the sun's half gone. It's time for tea." A raw
wind wounded. We'd roamed the beach and Castle Walk
and stood again on the town's prow. We spun
to tea above Portrush's rocks, talk
stopped before now bubbling. I was undone
all week by scenes that once were merely words:
The Coast Road tangling round headlands, shops
in Belfast, Stormont regal hard by herds
of ambling sheep. But pilgrimages must stop.
I'd seen my roots, filled in with real the form
of fantasy. I kissed goodbye the warm

12

found kin who, rationed since the war in food
and fuel, had shared their brimming meagerness.
I did not know before I would caress
this land again twenty years would brood
and simmer to another war, a feud
with roots a maze of twists in fired bottomless
soil. I waved back from the plane. "God bless,"
I mouthed, they mouthing back till altitude
cut clean the poignant pantomime, borders
of unseen air between our common space.
I married. Children came. Years obscenely
fleet dipped and swayed. Across the race
at Christmas time we exchanged cards, keen
at first, then less so. *You* know. "It's a disgrace,

13

Fred flicked the paper down. A child lay bloody
on a Belfast street in halftone black-
and-white. "Incident, indeed. A ruddy
war, I say." Fred's not British. A knack
for cuddling round a word or two that skims
the surface of a culture on his mind,
is all. "What's England *want*, or Ireland?" Limns
the sheet once more. "Children shot. Kind
against kind."—"It's not what they *want*," I say,
and stop. How explain a poisoned plant
whose roots cannot be found, whose noxious day
seems endless, air hung between us, dissonant.
Then, gently, Fred let loose his bomb. "I think
you'd like to see them once again." The clink

14

of a clattering cup blurred my caught breath. I stared,
touched. Stillness simmered. He'd sensed my need,
irrational, perhaps, but there, to lead
with kin the lives they daily led, backs bared
to insecurity and bullets, eyes pared
to slit to steel at every shadow, a creed
become a child's new catechism, seed
serumed with hate, shoots insidiously aired.
The last card said they'd thought of England's green,
transplanting there, and yet—Belfast was *home*.
...And from the South, "Christmas was rather lean.
I had to sell the place. I'm in a chrome-
and-plastic nursing home in Dublin. It's clean;
They're sometimes kind." I saw stiff lips. "Roam

15

those hills again," I mused aloud, the sweep
of Wicklow stinging my eyes. There'd be no stately
place to dally in, no lovely leap
through old, old lawns, of daffodils, sedately.
"Yes, Fred, I would." We said no more, but kissed.
Beneath his crust he understood the way
things inexplicably twisted in the mist
of lost beginnings, how subtly psyches sway.
I left in May and would return before
two children spun from college. Fred could not leave,
trapped in business tangles. I saw the shore
tilt back. A drink eased engines' recitative.
Oh genii gin, soothing parting's pace!
I twirled away to the other time. "The place

16

is kept quite well," my cousin quavered, straight
and brave, through shrunk to shell. I'd hired a car
after the usual rites that airports are,
and jounced to Dublin. My room was mellow in late
sunfall as well-mulled wine. Brimming the grate,
a fire licked spring chill. I'd dined in the bar,
a lively lounge, and groggy, bedded the spar
from space I was and slept till morning's freight
of birds stalled in my station. An expansive meal,
a trek through traffic... Nursing homes are the same,
Mississippi to the Liffey. Way stations... Real joy
crumbled her face at mine. Lame,
eager as sin, she pled with fragile zeal
to wander Wicklow and her home. "Game

17

filled that wood when we first married." We stood
on a rise, the manor below, trees
hazed in sun and seasons gone. "Tim would
never shoot anything, and how he'd freeze
poachers skulking for deer or hare. Thank you,
my dear. I have not been here since I had
to sell. It's not much changed, the sloping view
to daffodils glowing gold. No, I'm not sad,"
she read my face. "I *had* it, after all."
She limped, stately as the house, to car.
"You thought me cold," she murmured, "not knowing fall
was Tim's death date. Your bright spring life, so far
from fall, the contrast, I alone, still
lost... By nature stiff, I couldn't... You will

18

go north?" The soft side flipped to steel as we,
sun down, braked at the Home. "You'll find *that* sad.
I'm glad Tim's gone. We lived in the mad
post office strife and saw the South sing free.
That was good, but oh the gory legacy
of that liberty: death, a cesspool of bad
sediment boiling... Take care. The South's gone mad
to free the North at any cost. I see
right on both sides and wrong, and see there's no
solution. Sometimes I'm glad I'm old. My dear,
you've been a comfort. I need no longer go
to the manor. That's done. My living's here."
She would not let me take her arm, but kissed
me at the door. I knew an ending. Mist

19

smudged the coast next morning as I trained
north, the focus of my pilgrimage.
Would there be bombs at the border? Unrestrained
boredom hurried the guard who came to gauge
our passports' fealty, the innocence
of baggage. A quick riffling, a cursory glance...
So much for the lethal border. Evidence
of cooling fires? I dared to hope, to chance
optimism as fog fell away
to green serene as spring's repetitive shooting
here for eons before man's mad display,
and after. Lulled, I dozed. A tinny tooting
jabbed eyes wide to the approaching station,
to Norman waving, waiting. "No cessation,

20

no." Norman sadly shook his head
after we'd kissed and culled each other's eyes
for shifts in time, for things not said, the ties
that tether, answering my hope that fled
as I saw sandbags everywhere. "We tread
carefully." His voice was wry. "Devise
ways to circumvent Belfast, wise
to offbeat shops and alternative roads, wed
to vigilance constanter than World War II
demanded. There is no warning now, you see,
no alerting sirens as you do the daily ordinary. Cautiously
one rounds, in certain districts, corners, few
illusions as to safety's margin." We

21

were spiraling from the city as he talked
"You said you wanted truth not coated," he laid
a hand on mine. "I do," I nodded, gawked
at gouges where a line of homes had stayed
breathing bodies obviously blown to bone,
I do. I need to know. I was formed here...
We both were still. Truth was no wise old crone
spinning a people's heritage in dear
fey-fashioned tones. Truth was a bloody face
with fangs and empty sockets. Truth had a tongue
that tolled and whined and screamed and writhed..." The place
hasn't changed one whit, Enid," I clung
to facades, greeting her gray, her tired lines,
nerves nibbled just below the surface. "Fine

22

fissures here and there," she smiled. "Come in.
We've still one son at home. Dora's married
in Australia." Yes. The usual harried
Christmas card had told. "And Evelyn
is off in Edinburgh, teaching. Lynn,"
a tall mustached man with eyes that carried
warm and gentle fires smiled and parried
his Mother's pride with quiet wit, a grin
that hugged and tugged, "keeps me sane. Come,
you're panting for a wash and tea." Soon
twenty years were sliced away in rum-
flavored fruitcake, strong, strong tea, the runic
quality of spirited talk, the hum
of happiness in kin. "Tomorrow noon

23

(you'll want to sleep till then), we'll motor to haunts
of yours; Coleraine, where your brothers went
to school's been hit, I think. Sorry." "I want
to see it, need to, Norman. My whole intent
is to see firsthand hate's holy ends."
"Ends indeed," Enid sighed. "Lynn
sees endings in beginnings, teaching, spends
his day on tots with hate for blood and sin
seen only as the 'enemy' stoned and missed.
Enemy!" Enid's eyes were flames. "Babies
like themselves taught to namecall, resist
nothing understood...I tell you, we've rabies.
We foam at the mouth, beasts, and deadly dumb...
We must fight for peace." She stopped. "Come

24

to bed, my dear. Tomorrow you will see
hate's fruit." Lynn stood up, tender, tall,
sensitive and sad. "Forgive us all.
We have seen so much," he turned to me.
"Sometimes I climb the hills, stars floating free
in perfect skies and want to fly and fall
within their innocent light away from all
this muddled dark. But this is home. I'll see
it through. You know. The same skeins brought you here."
I nodded, knowing, loving this gentle man
of twenty-three. "Tomorrow will be clear,"
Norman glared at the glass. "Good, we can
pack a picnic tea, take the rearing
safer narrow roads..." Drained, I ran

25

as if pursued to bed. I had forgotten
the sleet-cold sheets of Ireland in May...
I woke at one (jet lag!) to tea. "When
you've dressed we'll go and pass Lynn's school. Today
he's taking a busload to tour Stormont." The school
was gray, walled, the bus joy-yellow. Lynn
waved as we parked to watch them go, a cool
wind pushing skies. The bus stuttered off. In
a second incised forever on the mind,
sound cracked all barriers: the bus blew up like hell.
Air was a maelstrom of fire and limbs, lined
with searing wails, the stuck horn like a knell.
Flew to our side like a faun bird, Lynn's hand
we knew by the ring, ends rivering red on the land.

from *Contrasts in Keening: Ireland*

II

after picking mint
    I offer you
        my fragrant hands

from *Star-Mapped*

IN TOUCH WITH THE CONTINUUM

I sit by a stream in the Pine Barrens of New Jersey. This is a branch of the Rancocas Creek which winds through a large portion of these rare woods. It is a sun-splashed October morning. Even the shadows of trees reflected in the stream sparkle. Birds spin, dip, turn somersaults in tanged air. Some soar over their drifting shadows. I have brought a book to read. I would almost sooner be caught nude on a major highway than find myself anywhere without a book. My writing pad's here, too. Both lie on the grass beside me.

Like the birds, I drift. To Maine, other waters, other times. It is ten years ago. We are in Castine, Maine, my husband and I, the community we have come to love, where we talk of retiring eventually. The Maine Maritime Academy is here. Berthed at the Academy dock is the 13,330 ton impressive training ship for Academy students, *The State of Maine*. As we enjoy lobster rolls and hot coffee, we watch students busily carrying out whatever their jobs require. I have been a college English professor for some years; perhaps when we come here to live I could teach at the Academy? It's a stimulating idea!

A few blocks away is the small but splendid Wilson Museum which my husband and I have joined. It is Bob's intention, should we move here, to work on a volunteer basis with the museum. It is a treasure trove of pre-historic material from Europe, Africa, and the Americas, and local Indian artifacts, as well as rocks and minerals. My husband always wanted to go on an archeological dig, but other things took precedence. Here he does it vicariously.

On one side the museum faces the sea. It is lovely to look out from the ordered stillness of the museum to the thrashing endlessly fascinating ocean. Sailboats move past, some going out to sea, some coming in to Castine Harbor. Inside, one is carried back in time to other cultures, to people who have now passed away. We like the sense of connection, the sense of being part of a continuum that is as natural as the gulls dipping for fish, floating on the water like toys.

After our yummy lunch (only in Maine are the lobsters so special!) we take portable chairs, a blanket, and our books, to enjoy the hospitable lawn of the grounds of an old fort which looks right out to sea. Lazily, we read a little, doze a little, dream a lot, watch the ships leaving and entering the harbor. It is a superb vantage point.

Bob always brings binoculars, wherever we go. A sailor himself, he does not want to miss any nuance here of what the crew is doing on a handsome sailboat. Is it time to put up the spinnaker, haul it in? He is vitally interested. We look at gulls and a rich assortment of other birds, close-up. Another world to enter. No. Part, of *this* world, our inter-connected world. We deeply feel the intertwining of everything, all things and creatures in the universe.

Here in the Pine Barrens my book lies unread, for today. It is my writing pad which has engaged me, as it frequently does. The Rancocas Creek flows on as the sea enriching the Maine coast flows on, all somewhere coming together, certainly in my blood, bones, marrow. Indians lived here in times not so very long past, as Indians lived in Maine. They hunted, made love, prayed to gods we in our "civilized" world seem often to have forgotten. Rain gods, moon gods, wind gods, gods of grasses and crops. Beautiful Indian names move across my mind as shadows move across waters: Rancocas, Penobscot, Cherokee, Piscataquis....

If I stare long enough, strong enough, into the stream before me I think I can see a youth in his feathered headband looking over my shoulder. Then that figure metamorphoses into the well over six-foot stature of my husband, who is now dead. We will not retire together to Castine, land of our dreams, land of great happiness in sea-sprayed summer winds.

But he comes to life in the never-ending stream, the never-ending oceans. You see we are here, there, he is here, there, everywhere. These old woods blend into the tall Maine woods. All one. Who can rein in the spirit which travels at will to the loveliest places we have known? Like the feather I almost see reflected in the stream, the spirit blows in the wind, earth-dust of these Pine Barrens and Maine on web and barb making a soil for growing, living things eternally to spring up, to renew.

Hello, my Pine Barrens, hello, my Maine.

from Travelers of Eternity

EARLY SPRING IN THE PINE BARRENS

Tentative syllables of green. I think
      how the whole story will unfold, think
how the pitcher plant I canoe toward
      in its room beneath canes of wild blueberry, network
of worts, will speak the climax in midsummer;
      how oaks will carry on and on, defying
denouement, the blank page after "The End."

Why is my father standing in the canoe
      like Jesus on his lake of lilies & listeners?
Father in his tomb of bones whole books
      ago? Summoned by green and words, Irish
father, preacher who wrote God on primroses
      and nettles, first chapter to last of his life.
Pitcher, preacher; words blend in the content

of this boat illustrated now by sun, birds
      shuttling over, shadows of worlds resurrected,
and me learning to speak again the litany
      hanging here like mists of his old land tangled
in subterranean roots to this old land.
      No monks in monasteries need translate, or tribal
chiefs: *earth, air, fire, water—*

writing to rock any boat, and do.

      from *Bluestones and Salt Hay*

Toward Healing

I

Across the marshy pond
       in New England, December light
              delves into shadows burning,

coldly austere,
       through rugs of ice
              to the sluggish bottom

where things/creatures
       fabulous and ordinary will lie
              in suspension until spring

sounding its muted horns
       moves (all writhings & squirmings)
              in a vast Te Deum, everything.

You are about to be born
       breathing in woodsy pungent essence
              and shades.

II

Two, I from my birthplace in Portstewart,
you from yours near that weedy pond, met
in the staid suburbs of Philadelphia, married,
set out on the mysterious wobbly journey
marriage is, in mellow prismatic autumn
before an altar fecund with apples, cornstooks,
shadows of birds flurrying toward winter haven,
loosing last summer songs *for us, for us,*
we knew, laughing, celebrating ancient vows.

You were a man who cast his life in the light
of invention's tree, garnered stars from the planet
of your own head to make new universes
tethered to earth by the steely strings of patents.
I was a woman amazed at birds of ingenuity

swooping from that tree into your hands
which could make anything, fix anything. I
was a woman who swam in the Milky Way of words
and music wearing the white swirl like a scarf.

But beats, rests, notes, intervals, dynamics
of creativity share a ground bass. We,
loners, creators, cupped hands round a cup of tea,
read our blended lives in the cosy leaves.

III
Leaves,
　　　　another metaphor,
　　　　　　　from our trees, separate
　　　　　　　　　　yet entwined as in an old myth

three sons
　　　　for all seasons, each spine,
　　　　　　　each veined pattern unique,
　　　　　　　　　　lithe, full-bodied

against the sky
　　　　alive in the streams
　　　　　　　of all winds, never pressed,
　　　　　　　　　　like the dead, in an album.

IV
One might say, *obvious as a crow on a winter branch*.
But this was an unnamed, unnameable bird
of total blackness. Utterly buried. Soundless.

What one would have heard
was the small coin of everyday talk,
would have seen the huge smile you wore,
that everyone knew, individual
as fingerprints.
Would have seen you at breakfast
taking coffee (milk, too much sugar),
brisk with the cat's shadow, it
indifferent on a nearby sideboard.
Would have seen you with me
at the seashore, five days before,
peering at waves,

discussing the inversion
that let mist roll in
like a blind let down.
Would have seen you,
the last morning, in the thirty-seventh year
of our marriage, fixing my eyeglasses,
I going to teach, you with a later appointment.
Would have heard the soft swish
of my bending to kiss you quick goodbye.
"See you at six; we're going to hear Bach, remember?"

Yes.

Nothing unusual.

Depression's a sly, despicable bird
wearing nettle-like feathers that flip, change,
a rotting bird of a thousand disguises.
Nothing like
the starkly beautiful crow.

V

Here is the factory room, one hour from home,
where you were working on something new, another
clutch of ingenious ideas culled from your brain.
Alone, far from us all who loved you, October
brilliance on the mellow land like an offered blessing,
your hand that I knew on every willing millimeter
of my body, took up the black horror I never knew
you had, held it to the mouth that gave me syllables
of kindness, caring, love, and blew away
those dear inventive honored cells, spattering
precious essence on metallic chilled machines.

Where did you get the gun?

Easy as buying bar of soap.
Ubiquitous and ordinary as toys.

VI

Black pond, fashioned from waters of my eyes.
If you had only seized the old invention

of communication.
If you had only had some patented instrument
of special vision.
If only
If   If   If   If

I used to wonder what Woolf felt as water
claimed that genius, weighted down her skirt.
Did air caress Berryman falling through air?
Did gases soothe Plath? Did fumes sing
to Sexton, exhausted?

Three years drowning, I
in the dark bottom of a pond, oblivious
to any life there, any eggs of possibility,
believe I know the sirening delights
of just
stopping.
Unresistant.
Lovely bubbles of nothing.
Lovely.
Nothing.

VII

My dear, how I would be untrue
to life's throb, to the themes
strummed in the universe,
as would you, had you been
unbattered by wings of the terrible bird.

Look, on a hill behind the pond
a roan-colored horse streams
across the countryside
once more fruitful with exuberant October,
kicks a clod of dirt
into the pond. It settles;
in the settling stirs
the oozy mud of my being.
Weedy roots sway against fish
not yet ready for winter's long suspension.
Sun rides on the long steed of time
a luminous path to the very bottom.

Walk it.

Gentling past my ears, eyes,
Basho's meditation after a frog's leap
into ponds of understanding.

   watersound

Ripples after silence.

"The eyes of the blind shall be opened,
the ears of the deaf shall be unstopped."
Another meditation.

Life, with all its facets and dimensions of hell,
is one sort of heaven, at least.
I put one foot on the sunspun path,
begin to climb holding, like a rein,
one single hair from the horse.
I breathe out bubbles of darkness,
catch one with a glimmering of light,
ride it to the shore.

Love, I may love again...

It is my voice which breaks as I slipslide erect,
a creature of words and music,
reformed, hearing faint horns.
There is another bird
on the branch of my seventieth year.
It is shaking feathers,
scattering stars of becoming.
It is deciding
to fly.

    Unpublished

ILLUMINATIONS: FISH

They hang under ice
as if asleep, in dreams

hearing perhaps
the sink of limb shadows,

from a miry womb, fantasies
of peeper eggs imagining what

they will become, fronds
moaning at moon-knock, a stone

shifting in something like wind
more like remembrance of wave.

Their heads may sing with sound
in that tingled glove.

It is always the way,
silence an illusion

like frost in the bone
already phrasing : *flowers*

from *A Well-Tuned Harp*

ICE STORM

the glazed hull
of a grounded boat
star-mapped

the single blade
of silvered beach grass,
its black shadow

sawtoothed,
will the telephone
wire withhold your voice?

delicately
a black cat crosses
the frozen field

in strong wind
the whole coated wood
creaks

sunlight: overture
to the music
of melting

from *Star-Mapped*

EARLY SUMMER

Wind picks off the last of the tulips' heads
that colorfully cupped sun missed all winter.
There must have been shiny days but coldness blurs
vision; grey gripped us and a vague dread

that crocuses would never find their way
through darkness and the eager worms, since we,
superior (we think) to the simplicity
of flora, question rebirth, our destiny clay.

Raking up detritus under the maple tree
we find the matted, tattered fur of a squirrel
and its whole skeleton head worked clean, pearl-like.
How perfect its tiny teeth small hosts hungrily

pursuing could not reduce to dust. We want
to take it for a metaphor as summer unwinds
its fragrant festive carpet. Does something bind
us to whatever force preserves a scant

bit of us? An important modicum
that grips, rips, grinds, won't give in,
emerges jewellike after winter's skin
dissolves as if a warming sun were medium

for magic, which of course it is? A lake
of iris ripples in the back garden, deep red
roses frame the kitchen window burnished
by shifting shadows. It set on a shelf, we make

a kind of god of the perfect skeletal
head. We'll look at it all summer as days—
so long, so minted, so daisy-fresh—daze
towards fall and fall to winter's hectic brawl

of too-much-with-us worldliness. Moonlight
polishes the little teeth. We pour
tea and listen. That's what summer's for,
the speech of creatures in the mysterious infinite.

from *No Home to Return to But This*

SEASONS IN SPACE

For Vermont—hard, lovely land

This is what I see:

I am at the door of a small A-frame house in Vermont, I am not on top of a mountain, but halfway up the hill. It is summer. Sliding away from my house are green expanses strung with wildflowers.

> the small shadow
> > of a single buttercup
> > > reshaped by wind

There are birches. I never saw so many birches. Their white legs spindle toward the sun, their leaves drift small pools of shadows over tall grass; a wind moves slowly. There are clouds. High white ones that move as slowly as the grass. Is one a reflection of the other's motion? There are only birds sending unique songs into this stillness. There is no other house in sight. I am utterly alone. I love it.

> The woodpecker's click
> > then an unknown bird talking
> > > somewhere. Stranger here, too?

I turn back into my house. The sparsely furnished single room delights me. There is a cot which is entirely comfortable. I sleep under an electric blanket. I am familiar with Vermont winters, though in college days one didn't feel the cold so much. There are two chairs, one of them a deep womb for sinking into, the other upright, hard as Vermont.

> on the old straight chair
> > a spider warping, woofing
> > > rungs together

The deal table top was found in an old barn near town, as was all the furniture except the bookcases. The farmer didn't want any of it. I can see why. It's no longer young. Perhaps that's why I like it; neither am I. The farmer brought it all here in his truck. He asked no questions about a middle-aged lady furnishing a small house, obviously alone. I like that, too. He lives his life; I live mine. No judgments.

> always alone,
>> the sun never hoards its shining,
>>> now takes in an ant

I brought the bookcases from home in the back of my ancient station wagon. Books spill out of them. I could not possibly live without the books. The deal table holds the typewriter I have had for 30 years. It works, speaking its own language of time past, links me with now. I need to see what it will say for the future.

> one fly on the "I"
>> swooshing it away to clear
>>> spotted vision

I go to the rear of the room to the two small burners and small oven. Over them are four cabinets, to one side a minute sink. This is the kitchen. I have only a few dishes. I need no more. I make tea, toast with marmalade, and a fried egg on toast. I can live without many things, but not without the English breakfast that sparks my day.

> in the sink
>> in dregs of water dribble
>>> one cloud wavers

It is a warm day, sun-webbed, but not in the crushing, humid way of another place. I take my breakfast out to the single step at my door. Two fat squirrels watch me as I eat. They do not run away. A chipmunk skitters under my house. I hope his home is there. I like to think of him near me, carving out his own place.

I toss out crusts. The squirrels come closer. They look at me. I do not move. They come to the crusts and leisurely nibble. Birdsong had become an orchestra, finer than symphonies, finer in a different way.

> the strange bird, nearer
>> sings an air for the G string
>>> Bach will bind us

Shortly, I shall go down the mountainside into the small village. I shall walk. This is a day and countryside for walking. I don't need much.

The general store has almost everything, and talk if I want it. Silence if I want that. I do, for now. That may change. But I think not. I have lived with too much speech, for the most part idle.

> the squirrel's speech
> rumors told by tall grasses—
> these vital vowels

from Seasons in Space

FANFARE ON CHRISTMAS EVE

ice coated
the dogwood tree twinkles
after a squirrel's leap

on starlit ice
the three-legged cat
skids home

the wonder
of old starlight
just reaching us

church bells—
the crackling passage
of expectant feet

    from *Star-Mapped*

MEDITATION: LOOKING AT A DUMP

Hovering over the dump a good distance
inland, gulls offer even that polluted place
a sense of regality. The eye, like a period
typed stark on white paper, finds something
redeemable in the smoldering heap, ignites
its host to swoop and snatch a modicum of—what?

Consider what we take for granted: their grace
punctuating reams of sky or beach where we walk
hand in hand with lover or found aloneness wrested
from daily mills, under their innocent shadows,
or near them as they move like small ships
with spindly rudders.

Stretch a hand up. Patience. They may, trust
established, take the bread, the shared communion,
screeching *thanks* or *more*, who knows?, the long
sails of their wings steady in any wind.

Were they different, residents of Salt Lake City
who erected a monument to gulls that destroyed
millions of crickets in 1848, saving settlers' crops?
Crickets are lovely in summer dusks, singing
soft goodnights, but the world is a ponderous chain
of greater good decided arbitrarily, or not
arbitrarily, maybe, another unsolvable mystery.

Who, now, would give them a monument,
these ubiquitous, beautiful, lyrical poets
writing stanzas of elegance over dumps
we make and make and make, endlessly
believing the blue globe, blurred now by ash,
to be infinite, extinction a word
in another language spoken by no one.
Dead, in fact.

from *No Home to Return to But This*

ILLUMINATED PAGE

The creek
speaks quietly beside
a silence lovely brimmed
with just belief, that creed
trembling on the tendril
splashing up from weeds
and greenly reaching.

I am moved to an assumption
of the daily bones and beads
of one scribe working
to set down the way it was,
am here to write
whatever sense may seep
into tendons untangling
from overshout and kill.
The swath of scene before,
around, me, is the margin
everything illumines.

My time here's too little
to understand the squirrel's
astonishing wingless flight,
his centuries' spring and hover
there on a twig of pitch pine.
Or bluejays, bluebells, sounding
like saintly hours
on the stare of frogs—
names of all the world
we know, held, still.

I think how the monk's
habit itchy with lice
and probably lust
held him to a discipline

of doves and gaudy riot
running round luxurious,
and paradoxical, trappings
of God. Matthew, John.
The Christ Himself luminously
sad, the scintillating
cross...Look, a human
hand's more comfortable with
less blinding visions. I think
the singing knots and links
caught in Kells,
the skittery wild and somehow
tamed yet never tamed
woodfey, bog-shy creatures
were divined as dance,
wine-inspired dreams in blood
too stately wedded, bedazzled
by spring's annunciations
and splendid blasphemies.

Now on my page a heron
drifts its shadow riffled
by wind, like the wing
of a god crossing, recrossing,
blurring distinctions, the weather
of something a man simply
scribing his life fired
into mine trying to find
an essential minimum.

The base metal must be
an assumption of faith.

      from *Bluestones and Salt Hay*

SINGULARITIES

In a 1970 survey, Dr. Jack McCormick raised to
800 the estimate of total Pine Barren plant species.
Vegetation in New Jersey

through the eye
to the tongue:

curly grass fern
broom crowberry
cotton grass
sedge, aster,
goldenrod,
turkeybeard,
pixie moss,
goat's rue,
American mistletoe,
sand myrtle,
bog asphodel,
Pine Barrens gentian,
goldencrest,
loosestrife,
milkworts,
violets,
orchids,
pipeworts,
greenbriar,
lobelia,
grasses,
rushes...

the tongue tangles
in the litany
of prolificacy
luscious as these blueberries
picked before breakfast,
frosted with sugar,
enlightened by cream.

and now the tangy trill
of a bird...

from *Travelers of Eternity*

SPEECH OF THE SOIL:
HOMAGE TO WALT WHITMAN

Ordinary. You barely notice me under your foot.
Only my absence would shiver your careless stride.
In my rock, mineral particles all
sizes mix with living things, their remains.
I am colorblind: in Georgia maroon as a perfect
claret, in North Dakota intricate nuances
of black. On the beach, holding reflections of birds
and you roaming its reaches for driftwood or renewal
of soul, or stretched on a blanket with lover or child,
I am white, easing silently towards the sea.
At once, I am womb and tomb. This is the message:
they are one. Out of me as I speak
the daisy, complex beyond saying, tilts tendrils
towards light, its roots flesh of your dear dead,
hallowed substance which will receive once more
elements they took (too casually?) on skins you knew
impulses of moon, stars, sun, wind
with its celebration of the globe's dialects, elegant
fabrics of snow, rain. I hold your tears,
transform them, again and again, into eye's vision.
On me rests what you share world with, weighty
step of a water buffalo in China, graceful
gait of a gazelle approaching a pool in Africa,
singular imprint of a heron adroit on one leg,
ponderous shuffle of a giant tortoise on an island
remote, rare, tremor of the spider's eight toes,
fragile, immense, reverberations still
of creatures held in the memory bank I am
that have spun in the sun their day and passed like the passenger
pigeon. I am their enrichment, an offering to you.

I can distinguish, I tell you I can, the tentative
touch of Eve's naked foot from the sandaled meditation
of Sophocles' step, or the throbbing, merry
movement of Shakespeare's quickening me. I hold as treasure
trudge of a coolie in China, the chained inching

of a black in early America. No footfall is lost;
each is sacred, a pitch in the universe. Listen.
This is the dream and the reality of
a man in love with all there is that we know,
whose passage over me, vibrating hugely, stays.

from *Bluestones and Salt Hay*

MORE LIGHT, LARGER VISION

In 1190, the Japanese poet Jien composed, in four hours, a 100-set tanka sequence on the subjects of flowers, cuckoo, moon, snow, love, pine, bamboo, mountain hut, sea lane, reflections—ten poems on each subject. I was inspired to do the same, though my 100-set tanka sequence, on the same subjects, took a little longer—about twelve days:

Cuckoo

is it held in the
thicket's tangle, the cuckoo's
song heard last summer?
this haunted feeling as I
wander the same, yet strange, path

Flowers

forsythia wands
brought in for forcing, forcing
      winter away, yes,
but forcing time forward too—
      always, two sides to petals

Moon

once more crying geese
cross the moon's uncaring face
      and I cry for time
ever on the wing, I with
      no home to fly to, you gone

Pine

a flutter of snow
from the pine tree and a flare
      of cardinal wings
yet I'm yearning for spring—why
      do I wish my life away?

Snow

this blizzard batters
house, barn, trees, huddling birds
      and the lone black cat
crossing the field, isn't it
      strange, it's made of soft white flakes

Bamboo

shall I measure you,
child, by the bamboo's new growth?
      but my arms won't grow
long enough, fast enough! You
      run off through the field laughing

Mountain Hut

I won't disturb you,
spider, for in this lonely
      hut, I like to think
I can hear you form the web,
      your lifelines, as I shape mine

from *More Light, Larger Vision*

III

eaves
    pulling sound
        from the wind

winner of the Eri Nakamura Award
Modern Haiku

Women: In the Mask and Beyond

I was fortunate to have been born into a family where words and music made up the air we breathed. Books filled our house in a happy jumble, along with various instruments and scores. Both parents were musicians, my mother a graduate of the London College of Music. My father, a clergyman, had a silver tongue and often quoted poetry in his sermons. He gave readings in the old sense: from memory.

Odd, then, perhaps, that I did not come to the writing of poetry until the age of 45, though I have read it omnivorously all my life, as others read novels. I seem to have come to many things late! Earned both an undergraduate and a master's degree while raising my three sons. Then, at long last, it was my turn. Perhaps the long delay was in part why I was drawn to writing about the lives of women, for women so often sublimate their needs and dreams to the demands of others. I am attracted to the persona poem, the dramatic monologue; it is a challenge to me to attempt to get into the minds and hearts of various people, in the case of this collection, specifically women. I was moved to attempt to retrieve some who have been relegated to footnotes or only a page or two in the biographies of men

Several of these women were ruthlessly, cruelly, abandoned, a circumstance as timely today as in their eras. Ira Dalser, for instance, Mussolini's mistress, was imprisoned in a lunatic asylum simply to get her out of the dictator's way. Annette Vallon piteously retained Wordsworth's name throughout the rest of her life. Marie d'Agoult, Liszt's mistress (one of them!) and the mother of his children, suffered greatly, but was able to summon the strength to write scathingly of the musician's defection. Each woman I wrote about appealed to me in varying ways. Here are lives I felt deserved exposure to more light. Many of them have never before been addressed in poetry. I wanted to bring them into the canon.

As for the art of poetry itself, simply, I love it, almost sensuously love words. I enjoy working in both traditional forms and free verse, just as, if one is going to be a serious pianist, one learns to play in all keys.

THE CAR

In Memoriam, Anne Sexton

Sure there were jolly times, jouncing to lunches
with literary pals, or picnics with kids all punches
and wisecracks (until you noticed their vulnerable eyes,
especially the daughters' reflecting their mother's).
    Memorialize
endings if you want but remember the lively lines
flung in a folder on my backrest under pines
after a workshop. What you don't know is they fired
my tired upholstery until I flamed, wired
to God, maybe, during one batch rowing
night's dark water. White sheets shivered, towing
their freight of need, rose up like offerings, I
the bewildered altar, blinded by the long cry,
each syllable a tear. Would I rust to ruin? I tell you
each trip was a journey; I often hated the view.
Back and forth to Bedlam I carried her, weighted
by all her burdened prettiness, she baited
by Death, his stuckout tongue, his chameleon-hide,
sweet as a lover's, in a second a snake's. Snide,
luring, clever, more steadfast than Life, that traitor
I watched play her false so often. Which was Creator,
which Killer? The question's creaked in my springs ever since

The moon sits in my emptiness. Sometimes I convince
myself she's coming to me, smiling, her gait
slightly whiskey-tilted. I listen. I wait.
But there is only the wind sighing its dirge
so like the one it sang when the awful urge
overwhelmed. Or was it Death whispering again
his promise: Come, *I'll keep you safe. Amen.*
What could a body, metal, brainless, do,
no matter its heart howled in the cold blue
afternoon for another chance, another ride
towards Parnassus? I cuddled her, choking, no pride
in my exhausted air that swirled like arms
unable to hold her, hold her back. Charms

sirened from another world always known, crooked
ringed tapered fingers beckoned. How eagerly she looked
into the beautiful terrible face. I heard
the bells she heard, the fairytales that stirred
but never satisfied. I saw her night,
her starry night and knew that was the light
she had to follow. I kept a single hair,
from it can conjure the whole woman bare
in her bones no matter what she wore. I gave
her what she wanted, a Saviour who could not save.

from Women: In the Mask and Beyond

KEEPING THE WORD: CHANT ROYAL

What though the dead be crowded, each to each,
What though our houses be destroyed?
We will preserve you, Russian speech,
Keep you alive, great Russian word.

And so nothing in the world
is stronger than I,
And I can bear anything, even this
                               Anna Akhmatova

Oil lamp. A curve of yellow burns night
on the Black Sea coast where you bloom into day
of your first breath. Mirrors hold the light
in walnut frames, give back light to play
on rustling skirts, plush chairs, a density
of old plaid rugs, a samovar, tea
steaming towards June crickets. You would confide
"the patterned silence" of your childhood, slide
the hurt into smoothest words, versing
how the voice of wind could override
lack, speaking to your understanding.

Christmas, 1903. Streets a white
whirl, you meet your fate on the way
to buy tree baubles: Gumilyov, polite
and smitten by your too-pale face, grey
wild bird eyes. He saw in you the sea,
you *in* sea, water nymph in filigree
of foam and deeper currents, saw his bride-
to-be, bride only after suicide
attempts, two, his florid frenzied offering
to love's burning, singed. You denied
misgivings, wed, flew to Paris. Spring
is always Paris, always poetry. Right
bank and left trembled under sway
of giants seized by Muses. Erudite,
innocent, sometimes dark as death, they
touched the tongue of Mandelstam, esprit
of you, to song, dirge, singularity

of words. Gumilyov named you witch. Not soft-eyed
son could stitch the jagged deep divide
that marriage was, and so the others. A thing
all wing and fire, how could you abide
the bars of ordinary, pinions beating?

And Mandelstam whispered *Cassandra*. Death your sight.
Or vision? War and revolution must slay
old orders. In dark mists of new, might
hammered hell on spines of all. *Obey*
or die: they died, not always dead. Not free,
a state more stifling than earth-tomb where tree
is root, and worms give back a hard-held pride
in leaf, flower and fruit. All too clear-eyed,
could you think of flowers, every morning
heavy with news: arrest, at eventide
a death of someone who once shared your singing?

"Half harlot and half nun." Human. Bright
edging blight, the common lot, but protegée
of Parnassian gods, you were sprite
strung on steel. Shall we speak of flaying
cold, hand of leaching poverty
that served black bread, tea rarely,
and sugarless, the trek to queue beside
a sleeted prison wall, hoping to slide
a parcel to a son blue-lipped, thinning
there an eon of fourteen years? How ride
winds of crushing weather? Such a suffering
moved you to the Cross, the bereft Mary
under stars of death gleaming coldly.
Ruin to Requiem. Dignified
in loss of all, you stand, luminous guide
to lived endurance in poems that throb like praying.
And boats go quietly down the Neva, glide
through willows touched autumnal, all stars burning.

from *Women: In the Mask and Beyond*

Ravings From A Mental Institution: Ida Dalser

I

Scribblings.
Harmless.
What can an old woman, in tatters,
shadows of her snarled white hair
like worms on the water-stained wall,
dark skin dirt-streaked,
babbling, do to anyone?
Disbelief is the bird
shadowing scraps of paper
and the half-finger-length pencil
they let me have.

What year is this? 1920? '35? '36?
Who can tell one day, one month, one year
from another?
Just a slit of light, like a dagger
they dangle to tease. No way
to seize it for stilling
my heart that crazily goes on
beating against bars
as if someone could hear.

Stupid old woman
to move over memories as fingers
moved over beads of the rosary
I told when I was a child,
before stones became cold, dark cobbles
like these I lie on,
stench of my own waste
the only incense.

Stupid old woman
to move over memories as fingers
moved over beads of the rosary
I told when I was a child,

before stones became cold, dark cobbles
like these I lie on,
stench of my own waste
the only incense.

II

Editor of Avanti,
he boasts, chest testing seams
of his uniform.
We're draped under the arch of an arcade
in Milano (when? yesterday? forty years ago?),
my slit-black skirt leading him in
to the moon of me, the real moon
tumbling through cypresses.

Buono, Buono, I dimple,
not caring for anything
but the animal flare
of him over me I imagine
will be like God come
to His bride

I'm young as a new grape,
as juicy.

Soon we stumble to the lake;
he's pressing me on the dark bank
as trees loose shadows
into silvery waters.
God's own rod, I whisper,
drunk on the drama of him.
Night birds blur.
But their songs are pure
music.

III

What matter he's married to Rachele?
He lives with *me,*
promises marriage.
My hands like feathers light
on the round ball of my womb, big
with his baby.
Benito, I croon,

like you, a panther.
He beams, centers his cheek
on my bare belly,
almost bursts as the baby kicks.

A panther. His hands move
to my dark fur. Large as I am
we mesh, twist. Outside the window
a star skitters towards earth.
Lucky.
I make a wish.

IV
Offices of Il Popolo
don't frighten me.
Here is your son, I shout
shoving towards him the skinny boy
with enormous head he made
in the hot nest of me
I scream, pace, threaten:
No maintenance money. MARRIAGE.
As you promised.
Anyway, I spit, *no money*
ever came.
Guards gag me, slap us both
half senseless, toss us
to darkness no straight pines mark
like points on a map.
Nothing to follow.
No way to go.
Hands, pockets empty
as withered pods.
Only this crippled seed-child beside me
rattling in hostile winds.

V
What does a woman have
who has nothing
but her voice? I raise it
in cafes and conferences, again, again.
Always his black henchmen handle me
and Benito like sticks of wood
they pile on a pyre.

I flame. They burn
us to nothing.

VI

To shut me up
he forcibly confined me
here. How long ago?
I used to try to scratch sunrises
on the wall with a hairpin.
They took all hairpins: dangerous.
To what? Who?

I am a lunatic. Am I?
My mind *does* wander
down strange alleys, pinched streets.
Where is the boy, Benito?
When was it they took him?
Was he real or did I dream him
flying out of me, an angel made by God?

Is that him in the corner,
eyes red as lamps
that used to wink *love*
on Milano streets?

Benito, Benito.
I grope towards the figure.
It bites me.
A rat.
I no longer shudder.
It sprints away dragging the dream.
The way of rats.

I embrace the dwarf-size pencil.
What does a destitute woman have
but her voice?

from *Women: In the Mask and Beyond*

IN THE "HOUSE OF SPECIAL PURPOSE," EKATERINBURG, MAY 1918: ANASTASIA

Anastasia was a charming little devil, such a bag of mischief that no one could ever be bored in her company. Lively and always on the move, she was continually pulling funny faces... as they do in the circus.

Eugen Platonovitch N.

Light's on the low hills. I know, though night
is our constant time. Stupid to let myself dream
tea and black bread will not be our breakfast. *May
and the lilacs are budding Tsarkoe Selo.* Time
for prayers, Papa calls. Quietly. Still, the guard
follows me to the lavatory. I blush. And hate.

Why do we pray, and to whom? How He must hate
us. *Oh*! I rinse my mouth of the dark night
of such sin. Olga's eyes are closed. The guard
leers at the door. I sway in the murmuring dream.
I am riding my pony on the curved track times
changed cannot steal, in the green brilliance of May.

Yes. Tea and black bread. But later we may
walk in the garden! However much we hate
alien eyes always on us, there is that time
of fight and birds to hold against the night
we wear like dirty clothes in a villain's dream.
In the garden even Mama drops her guard

a moment until her eyes lift to the guard's.
Then the Tsaritsa appears and the small patch of May
withers to winter. Where has she gone? Does she dream
of the mauve room she loved? Does evident hate
mask her drifting away to jewelled nights
in the palace, balalaikas keeping her loveliest time?

Behind my eyes, less cool than Mama's, time
takes me to my own kind of winter. Nothing that guard,
fouleyed and mouthed, can image. After crystalline night,
crystalline mornings. *Papa, dear Papa, may*

we make ice mounds? So we toboggan, hating,
loving the wind's cold slaps. Oh I could dream

down these days till I'm lost in my moans, dream,
dragging all with me. So I laugh, time
my queer faces for when theirs are saddest, hate
reined taut in every jokeline.... That one guard,
is his glint of compassion a mockery? Just May
madness coloring my sight, scenting the night,

night when I dream again. My spaniel runs
in another May, keeping time at my heels.
Beside me now, his breath guards, stanches hate.

from *Women: In the Mask and Beyond*

Meditation: After Singing the Verdi Requiem

for Guiseppina Strepponi

After the momentary hush, the applause,
the sparks challenging stars,
I went away to walk beside a creek in a wooded park.
Mid-afternoon; it had been a morning
performance, memoriam for a famous man

A flat rock, sunlit, alive with shadows
of birds, trees, and one great fern's fronds.
I sat on it, my stirred thoughts ran
like a current in the water, not to Verdi,
irrefutable genius, but to you
in your last moments apologizing to him:
ill with pneumonia you could not smell the flower
he brought you, senses and light beginning to dim.

Opera star. Stages strewn with flowers.
How little we know of the petal's underside.
You were rented out by an agent to any
impresario, without your approval, pride
pocketed for what you needed most: money,
you sole support of a widowed, illiterate
mother, younger siblings, your own child,
illegitimate, lost in history's footnotes.

Four or five times a week you sang, hours
of strain that ripped your voice almost beyond
repair, some married lover—who—a bee
sucking honey, offering no substance, flying
at dusk back to his hive. Your letters speak
of suicidal thoughts, withdrawal. A crying
flails the sunsplashed rock as if to crack it.

Seasons change. After witherings, awakenings.
Verdi dedicated *Jerusalem* to you
busy now with pupils. In summer's healing
light, together you rented a house in Passy,

with a garden: flowers, always flowers, theme
in the undulating opus of your life.

Verdi is busy with the grotto and the garden,
you wrote... *happier believing nothing,*
but you, devout, wanted the marriage of rose
with strong stem, wanted legitimacy.
Thorns rip even the silkiest salons of repose.

What brought him to union in 1859, who knows,
motivations elusive as clouds that, reforming, pass
from view. Threats of war? His decision to stand
as a public official? One understands (not crass)
the benefits: you could inherit as *real* widow.
No matter he grumbled, found fault whatever you did—
some days. Genius has its own unfecund plots.

The yellowing, the browning of petals, the turning years.
In Montecatini, he 83, you 81,
bent with arthritis, still, as a friend wrote,
offering "a suggestion of old beauty,"
he must have seen, bending, at the end, to kiss
your dead chilled cheek, his flushed, no tears,
then standing motionless beside a barren table.

No funeral flowers, crowds, or speeches, you said,
and so it was, and so I compose these reflections
for you, on a rock dusk chills, a Requiem
of Roses, fragrant, hardy. for you. unsung.

from *Women: In the Mask and Beyond*

For Verdi's Retarded Sister, At Their Father's Inn

                    Innocence
is its own miracle,
the one dropped petal
ringing ever wider
ripples, like a brother's sounds
circling, circling her stream
of consciousness, coloring the black
apron she wears standing in sunlight
filling the kitchen doorway, wild
garlic pungent in undemanding
                              hands.

from *Women: In the Mask and Beyond*

Mary Ludwig in Old Age

Whom history knows as Molly Pitcher

Once a year, like returning leaves, they come,
forty green dollars from the government. My hands,
no longer steady, clutch them: food, heat,

light for the small world of my room. I pay
them out slowly, slowly. A jay shrieks at the windows,
raucous, brilliant. *Why do you hoard*, I believe

he scolds. *At your age, be warm, eat well.* He doesn't
yet know how age devours courage and heaven
is a country I can't believe though I want to, have

always wanted to. Look, if you've seen war,
seen boys spill on the land like a legacy
for worms, you want to believe they've gone to God.

Nights, sometimes, I take a tot of whiskey,
neat. (Oh, never mind pointing the finger,
you in your warm mantle of youth.) Before

my scant fire the mind plays tricks with time. I
am as young as you, just married. I see
the beautiful arc of his body over me, hear

lovewords no lady should know, that I *loved*. We
whir to an island dotted with birds: maroon,
jade, cream. They sing us to the only heaven

I *know* exists. Then we all explode, he,
I, birds, island, in an iridescent
flash. We sleep. Everything's right in our world.

Hell. I believe in *that*. At Monmouth, the heat
sucked wits and marrow. What was it all *about*,
anyway? Revolution? *Was anything worth the dying?*

Maggots in boyish flesh move through my dreams
still. And blood, carpeting greeny June
too richly. Johnny, Johnny, I screeched when he fell,

and sprang to his gun. Without thinking. Burning. Furious.
For Johnny. I began to understand something
of how war invades bones like a madness. My hands

on the gun. God! It was power, kicking, whining, flaming.
Beyond anything known. Yes, I ferried pitchers
of water, heart cracking at how those boys panted,

sweat rushing down blackened limbs. Yes.
I did that, couldn't do enough. But the gun.
In my hands... I aimed to kill. And make no apology

for it. A demon took over my body. War
at the moment excites while it damns. (*That's* the hell.)
After, you weep in the gardens of bones, weep

that you could have planted some of them there (what matter
what side, what color the uniform), weep for what
you'd become... Then it was over. But it is never

over. My mind like a sleeping monster wakes up
when I most want peace, I, an old woman watching
leaves come and go, faster, faster each year,

who would like to think only of how it was when he came
to me first in the high hard bed, how his hand
round a cup of tea in the kitchen was tawny, and kind.

from Bluestones and Salt Hay

Soliloquy: Mrs. Magdalen Herbert, Montgomery Castle, Wales, 16— On Receiving An Epistle From John Donne

He writes that once more he is seized
by melancholy. *And bluebells ecstatic*
on the hills! Why does he hear
in church bells only chimes
of death? I could see coal dust
shrouding trees, ponds, clouds
if I so positioned the compass
of my mind. I look to wings
slanting to clover, swans believing
in living tableaux. *John, John,*
you must practice what you preach. God
may be more simplistic than your blue
soundings. Stand by the Thames. See
how currents accommodate barges, birds,
islands of human muck in the mainstream.

How light falls into fleece. A servant
showed me this morning a new lamb.
Think of that, John. *Think of that*
as you swill in thoughts of suicide. Nightly
I watch the first star trembling over
these hills, think of its bright shadow
here, on my hand, *there,* on yours.

...Shall I pen him this
springspurt? How I want to
shake his bones to burning out
of his pit. *John, sun is ringing*
bluebells. The timbre of primroses
is promise. I wish you could hear
these crucibled sermons.

from *Women: In the Mask and Beyond*

DIPTYCH: HARLINDE AND RENILDE

Daughters of Allard, Lord of Derain

With what foresight were they educated
in a convent at Valenciennes
centuries past when women were not fated,
(so men thought) to respond to learning?

With what foresight did they then renounce
the world that would not allow women's flashing minds
to flare beyond needlework's tame bounds?
See them at work in a nunnery at Maas-Eyck

writing, painting, deftly illuminating
the evangeliary found in the sacristy.
Listen to legend: while they were translating
inspiration to vellum by evening light

and wax-light, a cloud overcame them; a demon blew
the candles dark. Can you hear, through time
and civilization's bloody clamors, blue
night shutting down the world, miraculously,

the whispered breath of the Holy Spirit winking
wax-lights on, round each a radiant halo?
And the work goes on. Are you thinking
how demons and miracles were needed to explain

two gifted women's work? Still, we have it,
brilliant on the page, surviving both,
exposing both, the quiet, earnest grit
that gives us pale white doves, their moving shadows.

from *Women: In the Mask and Beyond*

Strong Against the Frost

Yosano Akiko (1878—1942) was a pacifist, a champion of women's rights, and one of the first tanka poets to be affected by new currents in psychology and Western poetry. She translated such classics as The Tale of Genji *into modern Japanese.*

I. Concerning Love

> my soft hair
>   swirls out in water
> holding the moon

> drying my hair—
>   plum blossoms don't speak
> of my sin

> dawnlight
>   in my air—I pick up
> my parasol

> honey smeared
>   on my lips, my breast
> flower

> will you be
>   on the bank of the river
> I cross?

> field of flowers
>   you are not waiting—
> this lonely fragrance

II. Concerning Peace

> thunder
>   I think of guns loaded
> with only flowers

> between the eyes
>   someone shoots
> a water hyacinth

dribbling down his face
　　pale scent
and petals

building a fortress
　　of rose petals, I listen
for bees

blood red
　　the camellia I aim
at a passing soldier

bombing
　　the white lotus
spring rain

III. Concerning Women's Rights

composing a song
　　"How lovely to be paid
in petals"

tone-deaf, he does not hear
　　what's on the underside
of blossoms

walking behind him
　　hornets
in my heart

I take the hand
　　of a beggarwoman, child
blooming in her belly

"deserted by him,"
　　she says, eyes full
of blacked-out stars

I write, write
　　of chrysanthemums, how strong
against the frost.

from *Strong Against the Frost*

IV

rose scent
   at dusk—
this catch in my throat

from *Star-Mapped*

AFTER A BLIZZARD,
THINKING OF PHILIP FRENEAU

There is nothing here but words, the calls we try the dark with—
hoping for a human ear, response, a rescue party.

Eleanor Wilner

Sun strikes
everything in the field
seen from the window
which yesterday was mobbed
by fierce cold flakes, angry
miniature militiamen, blinding,

so that I took the sure path
to vision, poems
from an older era when snowed in—
by firelight we like to think
was romantic, forgetting the hand
at the axe, the frozen pump.

Today, muffled as a mummy,
I tramp the tabula rasa
birds hungrily hover. Where
is the good corn, the offering
of rodent and root? Hard
to think, on this silent page,

of you, Freneau, furious
for liberty, equality. fraternity,
Yesterday's weather was more
your aura, you, violent
patriot, rascal. A hound
swims the deep white surf

at road's edge, *You patrolled*
the coast with your dog. You swam
in the surf of West Indian seas,
stank in a prison ship no rodents
deserted. How you ate roots
that fueled later print!

One drift, higher than my head.
Will I need a hand? I think
of Jefferson's hand at your back
nudging you to "a clerkship
in foreign languages," Jefferson
spinning out words as sun

here spins infinite prisms.
You saved, he said, the Constitution
when it was "galloping fast
into monarchy." Words that move
and moved nations, as nations
of light swirl, speak in my footprints

finding their way past drifts,
circling home. I stare
at what I have written in
the field, so still after storm.
You rise up on that glistening
sheet like a figment figure.

There you are in a deep
December storm, white
of hair, brittled by eighty years,
walking in the field towards home
when the snow's hard hands stop
your breath forever, no rescue

party near. But Philip,
here is an ear that heard you
last night when those knuckles knocked
at my window, too. My response
was to stay in the dark with words
that lead always to light, and save.

from *Molded Out of Faults*

MAINE: THE REAL SCENE

On the Commons in Castine a monument leans
its shadow dark with war dead names on grass
perfect as children's unhurried expectant dreams
of how the world is: summer will never pass
to limbs going bare before bearing, inevitably, snow.
In another direction grass runs to the home
tourists eye: Robert Lowell's. They gawk and go
to lunch on a sunlit deck where they may roam,
a moment, corners of his life, or what they think
was his life: chronicled slips into madness and marriages,
the circle of untidiness always around him, drink—
those false dramas, I say he sailed in carriages
golden, angel-borne, beyond screaming black birds,
beyond death and all dyings. I read that in
graven words.

from *Molded Out of Faults*

THE BREAKFAST TABLE, AUGUST 5, 1945

*The final decision of where and when to use the atomic
bomb was up to me. Let there be no mistake about it.*
Harry S Truman

We can imagine the table, can see
sun frothing over white linen.
There is perhaps a blue vase
joyous with wild asters.
Beyond the window a single bird shadows,
in fields sweetening Virginia,
you know there are poppies nodding, drowsing
towards summer's end, crickets
waiting in their dark suits
and questioning voices, for dusk.

Near the blue vase, sun
curls up in the lap of the silver spoon
he's uncomfortable with.
He understands steel, stainless,
simple as a Missouri Sunday.

What of the china?
Light as a moth in the hand,
precious as history.
Coffee, the color of rich farm loam,
puffs up a delicate mist blurring a moment
toast halfway to the mouth
moving to speak to a wife, a daughter,
cheerful greetings.
A steady hand releases
an egg's fullness.

In the grand echoings of the White House,
this room is amazing grace. You know
in another climate he would rush to save
bewildered butterflies just now lifting
to fire, sobbing, in their unbearable language,
of wings singed to nothing
beside a baby frozen
in charred skin.

You might want to weep for him, hard
as the bullet he's bitten.
You know the complex nature
of things, how miraculous the egg,
the birth, the blooming,
the pigment of poppies.

How long will he live, after?
With this.

A good man
at buck-stopping, caught
at a crossroads, vision fogged
by the heady smear of noxious cloud,
on his hands, on all our hands, ash
of midge-heart and child.

from Molded Out of Faults

Journal Entries Written by Light through a Princeton Window: Robert Oppenheimer in Late Years, on a Visit

Autumn, here, is always a tug at the gut
level of things fervently dying. Golden
light through mullioned windows pools on this pad.
I hear, now, in my mind the barkings of geese
as they swept over the river I walked beside
this morning in a crisp dawn ripe with color.
A small ant carried its freight of food—
where?—at the bridge a web's facets winked.
On the path I picked up a stone flat as a plate
and skipped it, skipped it across the shining water.
Matter in myriad form. It thrills, still.

When I was a child, oh, five or so,
I began to collect rocks. The thought of the one
winging this morning brought my assemblage to mind,
So many hues in hard! In shelves near my bed
they shone—maroon, green, blue, cream.
You have to be able to see beyond grey to bright,
beyond heavy to light you can hold in the hand.

Another autumn in Harvard Yard. Near
pebbles and structures of stone, universes of leaves
wind, chilling to winter, whirled and you wondered
what you had done to deserve that distribution
of atoms as you hurried to the warmth of the fire and wine,
the company of books. A wealth of distractions.
Physics that began to throb in the bed of my bones
like a constant love who never went whoring, or lied.

I must open the window, let the room fill
with tang, voices of birds dying to sleep
in hundreds of trees soundlessly loosing leaves.
This is not the evening I want to write
of Los Alamos, Fermi, all that galaxy of stars.

That's better tackled in winter's deadly drifts,
though I know questions hang on lips like nets
hoping to catch. Do they suppose questions
never trembled on *my* lips, the hive of my head?
Listen. Tonight in this wind of whispering pasts
I write only this: could the hand that fashioned the wheel
have stopped halfway to circle's completion? What hand,
in the doing, knows nerves exposed to death
on the trillion roads of time, raceways of worlds?

Philosophies are not facile. Nothing is
facile. My hand as I write is a complication
of cells beyond telling, or real understanding.
Mostly I think, now, I understand absolutely
nothing. This night I will go again
to the river's forgiveness where day has dusted down
on banks carpeted with leaf, stone, twig,
remembrance of geese passing on dancing molecules
over my head, itself a myth, moving.

A cloud stains the moon. I think how it was,
always in childhood's guileless harvest, uncluttered,
how its light fell clear on rocks, on the straight
path no longer apparent this All Hallows Eve.
Ghosts, good, bad, most men's mix,
sift from trees, knock at my window, pound
on the doors of my bones and I have a homesickness
for time no man can retrieve or differently draft.

                    from *Molded Out of Faults*

114

LAST THOUGHTS, APRIL 9, 1945, FLOSSENBURG: DIETRICH BONHOEFFER

Bonhoeffer was all humility and sweetness... he always seemed to diffuse an atmosphere of happiness, of joy in every smallest event in life, and of deep gratitude for the mere fact that he was alive... He had always been afraid that he would not be strong enough to stand such a test, but now he knew that there was nothing in life of which one need ever be afraid.

Captain Payne Best
imprisoned with Bonhoeffer

Come now thou greatest of feasts on the journey to freedom eternal; death, cast aside all the burdensome chains, and demolish the walls of our temporal body, the walls of our souls that are blinded.

Dietrich Bonhoeffer

Fingers of wind on the naked body seem
like the breath of God. I stop a moment outside
the cell, straighten to inhale the teeming
tones of birds like bells at Eastertide

in other weather, Guards prod us down stone steps
live with lichens still rime-etched in early
dawn. I think of time, the varied footsteps
stones have held: children's in games' hurly

burly, lovers' hurrying to a glade
or dreaming back to the mundane of beer
and sausages, all lovely promises made,
and sometimes kept, a hunter's bent on deer.

The scaffold now. The loop unmoved by cross
currents at foundations—shift of green
shoots towards April's promise, how weeds toss
heads patricianlike in wind, as lean

grasses in the mountains of my childhood
summers turned towards sun and we searched through
more shadowy patches and found mushrooms! I could
forever after tell them from the rue

of toadstools. How we tumbled in at dark
to baths and simple suppers. How we sang,
the brood of us, folksongs, hymns, last spark
of day trembling on a leaf. I rang

the chambers of my heart last night with prayer.
It was like lilies ringing in a place
I knew, an older garden. The figure there
knew *me*. I roamed the mystery of His face

and bones... Why in sweet spring air should I
think of Hitler? Pity any man
whose only climate is decay, whose eye
can never see in Jew, Jesus, human,

man purged pure, vines twisting, singing out
of flesh destroyed. I think of rich earth holding
bulb, root, and worm, under the stout
scaffold working. Now on this spot standing

stark and firm, I watch a bird climb air
till one guard takes my glasses, tethers wrists.
The trap door creaks. My vision clears. Fair
around me April flowers. All earth lists.

from *Molded Out of Faults*

JINRIKISHA BOY: JOHANNESBURG

Looks easily thirty. As a cloud darkens the dark
of his face, nearer forty, Why am I thinking of zebra

wild on a plain? Something has startled the herd.
They drum away from the peace of a small pool

on their rippling shadows. In the distance stripes whir to one
disappearing puff of grey, like a lovely smoke

against the sun. Against the sun, his face
now is full towards me. *Ageless.* Veldts, arguable

stripes (black on white? white on black?),
bones high in the sun-contoured cheek, lineages

of takes, coastal waters. Look they leap
in his eyes as I watch: snoek, pilchard, sole.

He is hauling cargo through streets far from his village.
See how his charms, his amulets glint, dazzle—

protection against city dangers. *White on black.*
Clearly. Sundown. Someone shouts, "Boy...

from *Molded Out of Faults*

THE DAVID

I hurry from Vecchio urgently, this hot day
fraught with ambling half-bare Americans,
needing to see once more the cool way
he countenances circling feet, amazed stares.

A boy, a youth given to fishing, maybe,
in streams littered with twigs and stepping-stones.
He'd lay down his pole, tentatively begin a key
on his small harp (always near) birds could tune to.

Ever I'm tugged here out of teeming streets,
art on every corner and in the Uffizi
that, too, calls and through centuries greets
austerely mobs of culture-hungry souls.

He slew Goliath. Never mind the slab
stretching towards the ceiling. *Just a boy
before a giant.* Something always stabs.
So young, so young. Sunlight mottles in.

I resist the urge to brush a cobweb someone's
missed from the naked toes, the old live bones.

from Molded Out of Faults

From the Top of the RCA Building

you tipsy out of the Rainbow
Room to the roof eight hundred
gulping feet over
the boroughs. To the left
a helicopter hangs
like a dun dragon-
fly over the Pan Am
perpendicular steel
stream. Pin people
glint like motes on skeins
webbing to water. A liner
toys past Liberty lustering
moth ball clouds. Here
you see it plain: the small
island taut between currents
whorling to sea. Words
spin from the statue in a tangle
of tongues. You tilt
back into rainbow, reeling
at the depth of perspective, the tricks
on the eye   on the ear   the huddle
calling their nameless names

from *A Well-Tuned Harp*

V

barbed wire, each hole
full of the ancient ongoing song
of crickets

from *Contemplations*

HAKUGAI: POEM FROM A CONCENTRATION CAMP

One hundred thousand persons were sent to concentration camps on a record which wouldn't support a conviction for stealing a dog.

Eugene V. Rostow

*T*he attack on Pearl Harbor on December 7, 1941, by Japanese forces resulted in a frenzy of panic on the west coast of the United States. 110,000 Japanese Americans, of whom some two thirds were American citizens, were removed from their homes and communities and incarcerated in camps situated in deserts.

On a sunny February day I visited the site of Manzanar Relocation Camp in the Owens Valley of California. The site is beside a highway. The Sierra Nevadas rise white and stunning behind the campsite. The mountains must have been a feast as well as a philosophical concept for people incarcerated. They might took to the mountains' ongoing existence after the little, often terrible, lives men lead. Or they might brood about free air, their own barbed-wired and watched. Cattle dung is clumped throughout the endless dust and wind shifting in sagebrush. A few concrete slabs remain to speak of barracks built on them. A remnant of a Japanese garden tells of beauty fashioned in a wilderness, more, of beautiful spirits who sought to wrest the most from their lot of little.

Although the camp I have written about takes the Manzanar site as its location, I have not written the Manzanar story. I hope I have written about what might have happened or been felt by those in all the concentration camps set up during World War II for American citizens, not a single one of whom was found to have practiced espionage, and out of whose ranks came the famed 442nd Regimental Combat Team, the most decorated fighting unit in the U.S. forces for its size in all U.S. Army history. The 442nd suffered sixty per cent casualties in the fight in the French Vosges to rescue a "lost battalion" of Texans cut off by the Germans—a greater number of dead and wounded than the number of troops saved. None of the 442nd ever deserted. This record was unmatched by any other American military outfit. We are familiar with their famous motto, "Go for Broke!" The equally famous 100th Infantry Battalion became the most decorated unit in the history of the U.S. Army.

There were at the time of Pearl Harbor four divisions of Japanese, not a faceless blob of "Japs." These were the *Issei*, first generation Japanese, the *Nisei*, second generation Japanese, the *Kibei*, those American-born Japanese who received part or all of their education in Japan, and the *Sansei*, third generation Japanese (babies at that time). The very old people in all camps spoke Japanese, probably exclusively. Chiyo and Kazuo would have spoken Japanese to each other and broken English to their children. The children were entirely American in speech and custom.

The two haiku by Issa, and "Winter Desolation" by Basho, are taken from *HAIKU*, Volume 4, Autumn-Winter. by R. H. Blyth, published by Hokuseido Press, Tokyo, Japan, 1952. The "thoughts" in italics which the old scholar uses for purposes of meditation are taken from the *Zenrinkushu,* an anthology compiled by Eicho from about 200 C.E.—books, still used by monks studying Zen in the monasteries, set forth by R. H. Blyth.

The characters in my sketches are fictional, drawn from reading, and individuals with whom I spoke. If by chance names of real people have been stumbled upon, apologies! Though the poem addresses a period of history, I have attempted to write a narrative poem, not history. Thus, some license has been taken:

This is our ancient history.

Rocks given to light
by a generous mother, earth
festive with forests fingering birds, sky
cut out by undulations of moths, bees,
butterflies, wildflowers holding their own
secret names in air
understanding the speech of rain,
wind, sun, moon, stars, and the silk
of snow, waters
and their annunciations
of fish, beasts
writing their own music.

People,
red as if singed by strong suns
long years, who did homage
to old gods,
pointing sure toes on trail
of buffalo, fox, coyote, bear,
speaking myths in the shine
of tribal fires.

The word was
abandonment
of old treaties, a bill
of Indian removal they paid
in a trail of tears
rivers of tears on a journey
to reservations where hands weave
in sun and the turning moons
old ghosts, dancing.

This is our ancient history.

Another page.
Waves, waves of skins and colors
broke over the California coast
a sound like assorted bells, speaking.
We speak sotto voce
or we do not speak at all
of acts accomplished there,
our progressive history.

Slaughtered:
Indians, Mexicans, Chinese,
sometimes honorably,
that is, by Law!

The Chinese Exclusion Act
bared sands
to wandering Japanese
who carried ancient knowledge
in their fingertips
for tilling, taming
obstreperous soils.
These soils bore fruit
more fruitfully
than lands labored in by whites
and this land of the free
murmured and then shouted
"yellow peril" and witches
in a new shade
were once more sought
for silencing.

Hysteria bloomed like
a vine that twists
all trees airless in
its tangling thrust.
Another Act, in 1924,
excluded the fertile fingers,
the flowing smiles.

Savage
only in knifing abundant life
out of resistant soil,
they were denied rights
of citizenship
who wanted only
what all men want:
to earn, simply, rice,
to love, to set light spinning
in a child's receptive eyes,
to hold the sun
in the warm bowls of their hands.

The "yellow peril"
were set up to be
the periled.

This is our ancient history
buried in pockets
of our plains and mountains
licked by seas surprised
by exclusivity, holding,
skin to roots, a mix
beyond belief, disturbed
by only man
writing
his ancient history.

FEBRUARY 22, 1942

Kazuo, the father, reads a poster on a telephone pole: "All persons of Japanese ancestry, both alien and non-alien, will be evacuated from the above-designated area by 12 o'clock noon on ..."

Five days. *Five days*
to sort and sell
a lifetime
accumulation—
my head in a maze;
no lane
leads to a clearing.

I won't see
the lettuce up
this year.

So, so—
won't see the
worms, either.

CHIYO, THE MOTHER, AND KAZUO, AFTER SUPPER

       Remember when you dug
       the pond?

And you clucked your tongue
and said we'd have no garden left?

       It was unwomanly
       to speak so
       to my husband.

M-mn. Don't cry,
Chiyo. The pond was
too big. Someone else
can fill it in.

       Ah.

126

Meanwhile,
let us leave our plot
weedless.

        Such long roots
        difficult
        to tug up all...

A SMALL BUSINESSMAN

I   ran a little store—
fruits and vegetables—
a living,
more,
a place for friends.
Mrs. So-and-So and how
her children fared,
or didn't, and wasn't the world
despite it all
a brisk spring onion
place to wake to?

CHIYO

Bitter, bitter
cold. We start
politely
discussing whose
blanket can be
spared to wall
the other family
out. Voices
climb and kick
the flimsy
structure.

The young husband
loses. His wife
will, I hope,
dutifully warm him.

How did we come
to this
display of stark
discourtesy?

CHIYO, ILL

I have trotted a week
the long space
from barracks to bathroom,
have given up everything
except the dream
I ride on waves of heat
shimmering from every pore.
The moon rocks in a tree
outside my window, a pine
in our garden
coaxed from clay

In that ship of light
I sail out of my bones
back, back, not
to our California cottage,
to a room of sliding panels
where my mother moves
her hands hard
fitting end to end
the rough seams
of life. I feel
the coarse silk of them
on my forehead. I am
six and sick and she
soothes with soup,
the recipe lost
long ago.

She flutters a paper butterfly
across my glazed eyes.
Its eyes (rounds of glass
stuck on, and winking)
prism my room in shine
and I follow that dance,

laughing, till I slip
to sleep. Waking, I am

well and my mother is
powerful as a god!
In my mind I follow her
down corridors
that mist to nothing.

Shapes shift
like smoke
accommodating air's currents.

I see her next small,
carefully straightening
though she cannot straighten
her body bent an the wharf.
America, America, she murmurs
and we are speaking of a sun
beyond our knowing
I will go to in a minute.
Her tears are that old dance
of eyes in all the rooms
of my body, crowded
with questions about the new
and the warm full
familiar flowers of my home.

She is the butterfly
after its short day
putting aside bright wings
for whatever comes
next, and I am not
well, and she is not
well, and the hollow hoot
of the steamer's summons
swords us through.

She recedes, as we wash away,
to point of light seen
through the hole
in my eye I hide
from all physicians,

a spirit moving
in shades
of every day and night.

The beast growls again
in the wastes of me
and I go
running, running,
in my hot mist.

There are no butterflies
in barracks bathrooms,
just roaches,
running too
in their dark dream
of some lost light.

CHIYO, END OF MAY 1942

We ladies meet to fashion flowers
in our special way, flowers forced
out of endless dust. I try to help
the old, who only know their mother tongue,
to English. *Branch*, I say, and break
at what I think's the crucial point.

Old veined hands show me why
the break's a little better lower.

So we build the beautiful together
in this desert place,
to make it bloom.

CATHY, THE DAUGHTER, JUNE 1942

Really, it fell in February
when our heads were tangled
in the maze of moving, feet
splayed in all directions,
directionless.

Who thought of birthdays? Who cared, friends falling
away down canyons of shifty-eyed suspicion.

Mom scraped up sixteen candles! Tonight
twenty of us watched the wasting wax
before I wished... never mind. We danced
in the dining hall Mom decorated:
origami animals! We laughed
like 5-year-olds at her frail fantasies.
I pocketed a paper mouse for luck.
Simple boughs, camellias from a plant
she brought from home and it *survived*.

Scratchy, needle sticking every bar, or so
it seemed, the phonograph was tinny fun,
"Don't Sit Under the Apple Tree" we hopped
and swung through my mind the crazy fact
that this dun-colored spot was once an apple
orchard swaying with warm fruit and scent.

...The word came in. "Break it up, disperse
to barracks. No congregating in large groups."
We raged/giggled bitter gales. We draw each breath
in groups and plot—only how to live ...

His name is Sam. He *is* eighteen and fun,
handsomer than Rob. Close-up, so cute.
His gift was a pin, a bird, carefully
carved, and by himself. Painted sunbright
and blue beyond this faded field.

I perch it on a bough in one of Mom's
islands of beauty, saved from tonight's
spy meeting, and prop it on the board
which is my bureau. I nest the mouse
there, too, perky on a stone
the shaped branch shadows. A purple mouse,
whiskers quivering orange!
Spunky spirit!

Behind the camp the moon props an elbow
an a mountain. I watch it slip through sky
before I sleep beside my family's breath.

KAZUO

Brave, I always think,
shoots battering out of brown,
no hands to help—but mine.

Cabbages are wise,
all head on spindly feet.
Squash are brawn, all body.

Beans, tomatoes, peas.
I hoe, snip, shape,
knead, coax

to purpose: family bones
kept straight, strong beyond
the daily mess.

The children each have plots,
penny-sized but pleasing.
More, source of roots.

The sunbird moves in my marrow.
Sometimes several hours
pass before barbed wire

rakes the earth of my eyes.

NIGHT SOUNDS

aaahhhhhoooowwwwwwweeeeeee
eeeoowwwwwweeeeehhhhhaaaaaaa
aaooooooeeeeeaaahhhhhhowwwaaaa

CHIYO

Kazuo will sleep all day
like the dead.
My good husband. Black birds

have pecked you to this, a man

proud of a day's long work,
now only puttering, puttering...

to what end? I must
paint out my pain—and his.
Today

our painting class will face
the guardhouse where MP's
snooze out their hours, *Why*

sketch THAT, I asked when told
the plans, I have that painting
done a hundred times

In your head, and mine,
in everyone's, but who
can slip those prints from

our heads to see the way
it was?
            Who will care,
I scowl at solemn Kyoko,

she devoted to teaching art
devoted to making it speak
beyond the pale canvas.

I do not know, she says. *I know*
we must record it... so
some brush blocks of stone

where one guard asks another
loudly, "What are those Japs doing?"
Does he think

we are all deaf? Or have learned nothing
of his language? "Straighten your cap,
Corporal; they're sketching us!"

"Yeah?" and Corporal, preening,
saunters by to see
if we can paint in English.

He eyes me oddly,
for I am taken, instead, by the way
clouds twist in trees and how

leaves say their singular lives
in lines of light and shadow playing
each surface differently,

Let others brush
coarse history
here.

The Corporal tables
his gun, tips his cap,
grinning.

KAZUO, AUTUMN 1943

We burn raked leaves
and watch smoke blur
the mountains. We

have been here forever.
We chat about gardens, slugs,
the fire spins orangey-pink;

we lean on rakes and taste
the old sweet tang of smoke
that saddens, its grey rooms

full of elsewhere autumns
and the long waste
to come, of winter.

CHIYO: JOURNAL NOTES, 1944

The summer passed as usual.
Cathy worked in the nursery
teaching tots, worrying—
oh didn't I know—about Sam.

Kazuo drinks a little more,
I think, after sundown
when the garden cannot console
and time's a stone bird.

Fred lives for Scouts
and I am grateful
for Akira's leadership
which keeps him in
good company
—and sometimes useful!

I paint, arrange
flowers to a pitch of perfection
they do not need
and move my family on,
trying not to think
of purpose or things lost.

We birth,
bury dead.

Our men move
inside us and we
spin away our nights
and days
and years.

KAZUO, NOVEMBER 1944

They called me in
to tell me to make ready
for release.

Release! I wander out
and pace the whole camp round
trying to take it in.

This bush I know,
these trees, some sort of roots.

Where will we go,

who will pay
for what?

How will they treat us
in that forest
of "free"?

from *Hakugai: Poem from a Concentration Camp*

VI

the stream
with its freight of twigs and leaves—
goes on

from *Contemplations*

HELOISE AND ABELARD: A VERSE PLAY
ECSTASIES & ADVERSITIES

*W*hile what I have written in this verse drama is imagined (there were no journals kept by any of the participants), I have adhered to the historical accounts, as the outline for my work, of the lives of Heloise and Abelard.

There are a number of translations of the Heloise and Abelard correspondence. I have used extracts, with some slight changes, of the translations in *Heloise and Abelard,* translated by Peter Wiles and published by Stein & Day, New York, 1973. Interspersed throughout these letters are imaginary comments by Heloise and Abelard.

Peter the Venerable's letter to Abelard, portions of Peter the Venerable's letter to Heloise after Abelard's death, the registry of Heloise's death, and a student's song, are versions appearing in the Wiles book.

At Sens, Bernard of Clairvaux worked to elicit from Abelard a confession of faith. This he was unable to do. It is interesting and telling, that it was to Heloise that Abelard wrote his famous apologia, the confession of faith no one else had been able to obtain from him.

PROLOGUE

From Orléans to Paris the Roman Way
Lay nearly straight stretching beside hay-
Cocks, tilled fields, vineyards foaming full
Down sturdy walls. Birds dove and swam in the pull,
The play of wind. Passed on the left, the church
Of Notre-Dame-des-Champs made quiet perch
For doves, below them, sheep. Off to the right,
Soaring over terraced slopes, bright
Planes of sun and moss cresting the hill,
Over it sparrows, their little shadows' spill,
Sat the Abbey of Sainte-Geneviève. Crumbling
Roman baths gaped wide to weather, tumbling
Vines and wine press part of the sprawling site
That spoke of Roman indulgence, eroded might.

In the twelfth century only two bridges led
Into Paris, a smallish spot spread
On former fields: the Petit-Pont, with churches
Spiring each bank (Saint-Séverin shadowed by birches
on the left, Saint-Julien on the right);
This linked the Left Bank. Reaching to the Right
Bank, the Grand-Pont spanned the river. The island
Glinted lucent, a gem on water's hand.

Bands of pilgrims passed on the ancient Way;
Merchants, too, tan behind the sway
Of pack animals pawing slowly towards
Markets and country fairs held in hordes
Anywhere between the banks of Seine
And Loire for fun as well as lucre's gain.
So the road, a pageant of passengers, led
To Paris, whose spires and clusters of towers fed
Young men's fires and fancies. Then, as still,
Her tang lured men sure of success by will.

Proud, expectant, Peter Abelard
Galloped to Paris on this boulevard.

ABELARD'S JOURNAL: PARIS

I cannot sleep. Sounds,
impressions move
in the mind like juggler's balls,

belled: The menagerie —
even an ostrich,
a camel that curbed my horse;

processions of squires, splendid
tunics shimmering
in sun. Paris at last,

after Le Pallet a pod
stuffed
with countless seed seeking

all manner of soil, light.
In this austere room
I lust for tomorrow's luxuries

of soul and mind, the chance
to cross
my wits with scholars', challenge

conundrums chiseled as if
in stone.
My head is a hive. Eyes

clink shut on the panorama,
giddy,
gaudy, all senses tingle —

Will the moon never
move on!

LETTER FROM ABELARD TO BERENGAR, HIS FATHER, IN LE PALLET, BRITTANY

Mon cher Père:

You with your passion for learning as well as arms
would approve of the schools of Paris thronged with students
spanning all ages, their animation and ardor.
New words, unfamiliar sounds fleck air
like flies; declensions, derivations are drilled
as styles score waxen tablets. Pens plume parchment.
Calculations crowd some minds. Strings
strung over wooden bridges are plucked to play
strange harmonies. Diagrams are maps
to musical notation. Some search the stars,
others plants, some scan the human skeleton.

I tilt and joust with those who seriously
and subtly debate, argue fine-edged distinctions.
Dialectics devours blood and brain. I sit,
so far still, under my idol William
of Champeaux, but soon I must speak out,
refute ideas set forth as fact, with logic
differing from his. I am audacious, Father,
you well know, and independent, fearless
in fighting, twisting like spider's silk through points
ill made. He must define his terms more clearly!

I write to do away with rumor, to
deploy your dissertations on a student's
station relative to a famous teacher's.
Save exhortation. You should know now
I cannot change my nature more than a star
in its set course.

        Beyond all this, I am
well, have sufficient food, I suppose,
not given to nurturing flesh; a bed I rage
to have to use the wasted hours of sleep!—
and all Paris spread like light that burns
while giving sight... May God keep you well,
Father, and to my Mother, solicitude.

              Peter

ABELARD'S JOURNAL, SOME MONTHS LATER IN LE PALLET WHERE HE HAS RETURNED AFTER A NERVOUS BREAKDOWN

Sun waters down the wall, I love
this garden
where I played, a boy

pampered and punished in
a delicate balance.
The same nests seem to nudge

leaves of old trees, vines
singing sweet,
beyond, fields wind-feathered.

My mother sorts her silks
thinking
I do not know she watches

every shift of muscle, even
my spirit's click,
how my mind shuttles

in and out of thought:
Melun, royal city
was a success, my school

regarded highly over the critical
tapestry France is, pupils
crowding like fingerlings in spring.

But I was after larger bait: established
rival to my old master
the catch I craved. I moved

my school near Paris, and Corbeil
spun with stimulation. I
collapsed. Nothing, a mere
pebble
on the path. Some called it

nerves. *Nonsense*, a slight
decline, a chance
to see Pallet once more, parents,

reshape my strategy,
attack
another way. Mother,

your quick eyes quiver.
You know
my plans are laid and I

will leave inside the week
your unsaid circle
of caring, healing habits.

Meanwhile, how finches flick
their golden song in
and out of sun-spattered leaves

HELOISE'S JOURNAL: FULBERT'S HOUSE

how we dally down the days
and nights   sometimes I stare
at stars, shivering   perfect
happiness belongs to them, the moon,
sun, flowers
and four winds, not men

then I see
we have become
stars, two points of light
merged as they fall
across the sky   clearly
luminescing clay

ABELARD'S JOURNAL: FULBERT'S HOUSE

God! We were
whirling,
I inside her, flaring

like suddenly fired
corollas when
Fulbert stalked in

on us, Mars and Venus,
bare.
His jaw fell slack as the dead.

His eyes stuck on her breasts
taut beneath mine,
on tangled tossing forests.

He stumbled off,
lacerated, surely,
in his loins.

We moaned apart
and dressed,
too languid in love to think

clearly.
Is it possible
he did not know?

Yet if he did, *why*
wait till now to order me
from his house?

Oh the agony of lovers faced with separation...

HELOISE'S JOURNAL: BRITTANY,
AFTER PETER'S RETURN TO PARIS

I cannot make him understand, who is
so brilliant he burns! Marriage would be error.
Error horrible as hell, grievous as God
hanged! Uncle will not remain dumb.
Never! We would be fools to believe it. Yet
Peter prattles, "I'd lose few clerical privileges,
nor would I forfeit my stall. Why, I could be
Pontiff in Rome with you beside me." I blush
at his naiveté.

                    Fulbert *will* talk!

But—beyond all this, and this I cannot
make come clear as water poured from a spring,
he is *not* common as any Canon crowding
Notre Dame! I quote Jerome, St. Paul;
marriage—de tanto matrimonii jugo—
and he, one of a community of spirits
made perfect, of noble souls, must choose the superior
state. It is the ideal, the gown of glory
he must choose. He pays a price for greatness.

I cite him all the dailiness of marriage
in a missive. I cite it here, the better
to remind me never, never to marry
Peter Abelard, my love, my madness.

....The pulings of a newborn child at midnight,
croonings of a nurse to quiet it;
hither and yoning of a household staff,
the filthiness of early infancy....

Peter, philosopher and scholar, think
of the hardship such a hive would work on you.
Could you write books while being stung with sound?
—But see, the wealthy manage, you will say—
Indeed, in apartments set apart, money
silently moving the spindles of everyday.

Peter, brilliant fool,

philosophers have little lucre,
and should you push for worldly gain,
time for philosophy and Scripture study
would fly like swallows south, no matter
what the season.

What I cannot write
is how, in time, he would hate
me he loved as heat loves fire
as sun loves the sky it must move through
as water loves the bed it travels.

O no, Peter.
Peter Abelard, you were meant for more
than marriage.
You are the world's treasure. I would lack
any sense to think you were,
could be
content to be merely mine.

I quote you Cicero, Theophrastus, Seneca,
Nazarites, Pharisees, Sadducees, Essenes,
bid you consider Socrates.

My dear obstinate Peter! What I cannot make
you see is that my love for you is perfect
free
unconditional.
I could not bear it chained
and common. I want you
you
alone.
My love transcends my self.

Peter, I moan across the miles to you,
this marriage would mean ruin!

This is the one action which will destroy us both
surely, and open the way
to sorrow great
as our love.

Peter, Peter, this marriage would mean ruin!

THE SEINE SPEAKS

I fold into myself and out, the same
as through past centuries' panoramas, tame
and turbulent, lips caressing banks, the island
jeweling my center. A lusty stand
of trees stood there before the regal church.
I took felled leaves and shadows' moving search
to heart, and then the cruse of human cries
for God the great church poured in pity, wise
and tolling vision beyond men's lives, their small
scurrying ways.

                                  Last night the tremor and bawl
of Notre Dame's bright bells broke on my skin.
From a high parapet
                    a man
                    leapt in.
My limbs rippled, but whether he sank or swam,
my depths are dumb. I heard from Notre Dame
howls as from hell, then shouts, clattering feet,
windows opening, whisperings and fleet
fires singeing skies before dawn lit,
as always, banks, island, all the spit
and shine of men.

                              But I have heard all this
before, and will again. The edifice
noise thunders through this morning lies stately still
across my corpus flowing on. It will,
a thousand years beyond, not matter that
this turmoil dips and sways, veriest sprat
in time, time eats. I fold serenely in
and out, absorbing good and stinking sin.

ABELARD'S JOURNAL

Her missive is like healing
herbs after
the poison, the knives

of St. Gildas. I love her.
Lord, she is
the skin I breathe through

daily, deeper now
than when our skins
like clouds moved into,

over one another
bright with sun and blue
birds.

All that is gone. We live
more lives than one
before we die

to God's endless skies,
and I must help her see
the final fruit of earthly vineyards.

She must be directed to God, and I
must write
most carefully...

I will attempt it
here
before its final form

We have made God our world. If I have not sent comfort or other
word to you, the cause lies in your prudence, not in my own neglect.
I trust your prudence, one of your strongest traits. It never crossed
my mind that you would need assistance, you whom God has dowered
with gifts of grace and goodness, whose word and example shine light
into troubled minds, who sustains the faint, whose breath fans into
fire the lukewarm.

It is her strong soul
that must be directed
properly. She is Christ's bride,

I must point out, the bond
before which all others
fall

away, mere motes
in strongest light

ABELARD'S JOURNAL: HE IS NOW AT ST. GILDAS

To be Abbot here is like
being Abbot
to a tribe of savages,

scurrilous over desolate
landscape, treeless,
rockbound, the sea cold and clacking.

My lovely oratory
built with love
and by our hands

stands stark to weather,
a rookery
a rabbit-warren now, perhaps.

The sole warmth
in *this* place
is the thought that soon

Heloise and her Sisters will live
there. Thank God
I can give her a home,

my wife, adrift and poor.
I can see
how she will thicken thatch,

adorn with her woman's touch
and wildflowers,
the chapel altar, how she will till

and farm the ground I love.
Oh, if I could go
as Abbot to that cloister—

the Paraclete—mine and hers,
leave this wandering
and isolation.

She would care for me
and I
for her...

          cold crackles our skins
after the happy probing
of forests for greenery.
          Sister Adelaide, I sniff,
turns out her special wheaten bread
          from meal the Count of Champagne sent.
          Old wine waits,
fat hares turn (I could not eat
our ducks I know by name!)
          what excesses
          for your birth day, Christ
we laud!
          The good Archbishop of Troyes
          (bless his soul) sent tapers for this feast,
          and Abelard, dear spiritual advisor,
          sent a new hymn.
One hundred and forty, now, for our use
          exclusively! How he loves song.
I never regret putting Sister Christine
          whose voice must make angels pout
          (if angels ever sense
          the sin of jealousy)
          in charge of singing, in charge
          of novices, too, by Peter's Rule.
"She will teach the others to sing, read, write, and
set down music; she will also take charge of the
library, lending and recovering books, and will look
after manuscripts and illuminations."

Did Peter think of *time*
when scribing that? No matter,
Christine is capable
          of all, more,
          loves the doing.

The Paraclete is all scents and singing
at this time!

Joy is grace, I think.

I try to maintain measure; strive that our vows may
uplift us to the Gospel's level, yet not exceed it.
We have no wish to be *more* than Christians.
            So I daily strive, with Abelard's constant counsel.
My great joy is his work
            he shares with me. Last week his six plancti. Oh—
his brilliance is unstopped. I cried over
his achievement, knowing these poems touch
            lightly as tapped bells on experiences
            we suffered...

            So, Abelard, you have not quite forgot
Heloise the woman
for Heloise the Abbess. No more have I
            forgotten your face
                        over me
                                    in passion. I see,
            sometimes during Mass, your shape
in lovely lewdness...

I should burn this!
God! will I always sin?

EPILOGUE

A chill necrology contains the end
of Heloise, in May. Words commend
her life: "First Abbess, Mother of our religious
order, renounced," the stark words go on thus,
"for her learning and piety, having given
us hope by her life," that life hard shriven,
"blissfully rendered up her soul to the Lord."

And was it blissful? Death an earned reward
for twenty years lived after Peter? She died,
as did the person of her love, her guide
through all and every thing, at sixty-three,
the same age, records clearly show, as he.

One makes no more of that, whether fate
or God or love's fine hand decreed the date.

We know they sleep at Père Lachaise together
linked in earth and by love's lonely tether.

We know old Roman ways still wander France
and alders over the Ardusson still dance
their shadows in the stream a great man, cut
in heart and body, built beside, a hut
that housed his dearest love, in need, as he,
of home and peace. Birds psalm a litany
in song and life in abbeys centuries touch
and fall away from calmly. Humans clutch
at life, or don't, and leave. All moves on,
a tapestry of threads random drawn.

And out of teeming time love touches, stills
the heart a while, the movement of the mills
that daily grind us down. Look up. A dove
cracks open clouds. Stars spill, defining love.

from *Heloise and Abelard: A Verse Play*

VII

this morning
a gold maple leaf
drifts to my doorstep

from *Contemplations*

OUT OF DARKNESS

*T*he urge to tell tales, to give news of the community, however small the community, to voice philosophical musings, to say poems, is as old as humankind.

The urge to set down such things in some kind of permanent medium is as ancient; cave paintings/writings tell us that. As more sophisticated means of writing evolved, so the inborn need to communicate embraced those means.

But the non-mechanical processes of writing remain as mysterious as they are profound. What forces nudge, nay often compel, people to spend long lonely hours setting down things no one other than family or friends may ever read?

Peter Abelard, the famous French scholastic philosopher, teacher, and theologian (born in 1079) wrote to Heloise, his great love, "Against the disease of writing one must take special precautions, since it is a dangerous and contagious disease."

Indeed the urge to write sometimes seems like a disease that takes over body and psyche with astonishing virulence. Indeed it appears to have contagious elements. Why else do writers' "groups" and "clubs" proliferate like toadstools after rain? Writing is of all pursuits the most solitary. One can paint with other people, sing with other people, dance with other people, but one must write alone, with enormous concentration.

Surely, then, people must think that they will "catch" writing in a group, as one catches measles. Summer writers' conferences are more popular every year. "How do you do it?" is both the covert and overt question assuming air, whether in Vermont or California. Rule No. 1, which is also Rule No. 9,999, that you go home, or somewhere, sit in a room by yourself, and push mind and pen, is the axiom least likely to be believed. Certainly there must be a magic key; if one finds it all doors will unlock!

Because writing *is* such a solitary affair, the social warmth of such groups must certainly be a factor, but the real writer, after two or three days, gets edgy and aches to go back to his/her solitary state needed for the pursuit of that strange business, writing.

Mary Roberts Rinehart in her book, *Writing is Work*, tells of "listening, too, for the postman's ring, and, from the top of the stairs, seeing him hand in the bulky envelope, addressed in my own writing, which told of a story coming back. Taking it with a sick feeling of discouragement, putting it back into the desk, and then beginning all over again."

Which about says it for all writers.

But why? Why begin all over again? Why not forget it and chase butterflies, or a golf ball, or any number of other things, than go through the masochistic hell writing is for most writers?

Mrs. Rinehart, of course, went on to great fame. Alas, very few of the myriads who take up pen or typewriter or word processor will have such good fortune. Most would-be writers, after rejection upon rejection, finally give up and turn to tatting—or something.

If they are successful (in whatever way you define "success") it is easier to understand why people continue the lonely, masochistic process. For some of us, "Fame is the spur," as Milton said. And, as Alexandre Dumas *père* stated, "Nothing succeeds like success." Perhaps.

On the other hand, William Faulkner said, "Really, the writer doesn't want success… He knows he has a short span of life, that the day will come when he must pass through the wall of oblivion, and he wants to leave a scratch on that wall—Kilroy was here—that somebody a hundred, or a thousand years later will see."

The "scratch on the wall" implies publication, which is a certain kind of success, the only kind beginning writers want. One assumes Faulkner meant: doesn't want *acclaim*, but wants to leave a body of published work for posterity.

I am intrigued by those who find little or no worldly success or publication, and yet write on, and on and on, to the ends of their lives. Particularly, poets interest me.

Almost everyone seems to write verse, if not poetry. Most of those who write it do so to catch a moment, or moments, in their lives. Family, a few friends, may be their only audience; most do not pursue the art with any sense of commitment, and commitment is essential to even a modicum of success, as William Stafford points out in his book *Writing the Australian Crawl*.

How many drawers of the world, then, are lined with unseen poems?

Emily Dickinson is probably the best-known poet, enormously prolific, who wrote despite a world deaf to her voice. Gerard Manley Hopkins was not discovered as a poet until about thirty-nine years after his death. One of the literary world's great astonishments was the finding of the work of poet Thomas Traherne, two centuries after his demise. John Donne's poems were published posthumously and were then promptly forgotten until 1912 — 300 years later. Edward Taylor, generally acknowledged to be, with Anne Bradstreet, colonial America's finest poet, died in 1729. His manuscript volume of poems was almost unknown until the 1930's.

What forces keep some people writing? Fame, obviously, for some is *not* the spur. What, then, is?

To quote Faulkner again, "The writer's only responsibility is to his art. He will be completely ruthless if he is a good one. He has a dream. It anguishes him so much he must get rid it it. He has no peace until then. Everything goes by the board: honor, pride, decency, security, happiness, all, to get the book written. If a writer has to rob his mother, he will not hesitate; the 'Ode on a Grecian Urn' is worth any number of old ladies."

Is that it? A dream to be captured no matter what? Faulkner was writing after having achieved "success." What would his attitudes have been had his work been continually rejected?

How important *is* recognition to a poet?

from *Out of Darkness*

LETTER FROM AN EDITOR

Dear Gerard Hopkins:

Though I am months behind in acknowledging submissions and haven't time for personal comments, your batch of poems just read suggested more than the standard printed rejection slip, because of a certain exuberance.

I had better begin with that exuberance. I have no way of knowing your age, but I assume you are very young, a student just attempting poetry. Your love of life is splendid, an asset you need now to harness a hard craft, should you decide to continue in a difficult medium. We must always distinguish between unstudied self-expression and poetry. It is admirable that you glorify God, as, for instance in the poem, "Pied Beauty," but to begin a poem, "Glory be to God," is self-indulgent. Emotion should be underplayed, not blasted in our faces.

Adjectives are the weakest part of speech. This same "Pied Beauty" fairly sizzles with the same. Consider: "dappled," "couple-color," "brinded" (a word I cannot locate in my lexicon). "Fresh-firecoal chestnut-falls"—obscure and excessively alliterative, as is "fickle, freckled, swift, slow, sweet, sour ..."

I cannot begin to address "The Windhover," which embodies all of the above faults: superfluity of adjectives (I suggest you go through your poems and take out every adjective. Lean bones, bare as a winter branch, will become visible), superfluity of alliteration (daylight's dauphin, dapple-dawn-drawn Falcon), senseless phraseology, unclear words.

Felt love of God and your extreme youth (an assumption on my part which must be a reality), plus the exhibited sincerity, have moved me to write at this length. Love of words is not sufficient; talent is essential. Think on these things.

I return your efforts with thanks.

from *Molded Out of Faults*

VIII

where his coat hung
the long empty nail,
its longer shadow

from *Star-Mapped*

A Brother Dies Of Lupus

He had no heritage of wolves.
Lambs, and fish prancing,
a cat holding blown clouds
in eyes the color of grass.

The double helix is a forest
of feasibilities. Look
how my hands are not Holbein's,

only my own stroking
the tamed peregrine, or bitten
by packs of mad dogs.

There were no howls to hear
thin on crystalline air,
shattering even strong limbs.

The single one first, silhouette
stark against the sky. You
might even offer it meat, a bed.

Satisfaction is nothing
understood. The hill beyond the hill
is the one wanted, it

already dissolving
to the one ahead.
Meat, bedding, never enough.

Reserves were called up, yowled
down the coil: *more, more*
fanged out on frosted breath.

The feast was an orgy
of organs: liver, kidneys,
the tasty heart.

We suppose them to have slunk
back. We think we hear them,
nights, in wilds of spiral,

whimpering they're still hungry,
why don't we feed them.
And someone will,
someone will.

from *A Well-Tuned Harp*

WATCHING SAILBOATS

For another brother, a minister

There's something clean about sailboats.
Shipshape, trim, those orderly adjectives

we can rarely apply to life. I watch
white triangles stagger and hold. Why

is *loss* the word identifying class
even at this distance? I see you

anchored and happy, wetting a line
for anything that flashed in scaly flesh.

You never believed in rowboats
for fishing. No. You wanted to sail,

tacking hard to deeps
you believed in, reeling slowly

surely, overcoming luffs, snapped masts
breaking brittle as the heart

we never knew, you never said,
was faulty as a flawed centerboard.

The sudden sinking. Quiet. No storm,
except for ours howling *no no*

to indifferent winds that take
whatever they can get for fuel.

In this circle of pines and sea
I hold your narrow volume of poems.

All about fishing. How you believed
a star could hook men to heaven.

from *A Well-Tuned Harp*

NEAR MISS

Lolling in a tub, languid
as Marie Antoinette before the fall
I idly soap the familiar
arrondissements of my body.

What is the strange small hill,
quite new in this district,
on the promontory
of my left breast?

Fleet as rain slithering down
a pane
I consult inspectors
green-gowned as doctors.
Out of place, they pronounce.
No permission given for this project.

> Is this structure a cancer
> obstructing all avenues
> of escape?

> Who is weeping
> into the wind
> all the way, all the way
> home?

Then the removal machine
I am sure will gape a hole
ugly, untouchable.

When I return
from a foreign country
an angel is whispering.
She translates:
benign, a blessing
I swallow, feel its fire

burn me to life
I tongue like a new lover.

inside my nifty negligee
whose label is *joie*
I pin a note for remembrance:

black smoke can smother.
Like that. Just
like that.

from *A Well-Tuned Harp*

CELEBRATIONS AND ELEGIES
FOR A FRIEND DEAD OF AIDS

the patio party
where we meet—how Venus
flares in white wine

attracted to you
before I know you can't...
you pluck me one rose

invited
to your studio—stopped
by one camellia
in oils

the strong erotic
headiness in all your art—
you brew herb tea

learning how deep
sexless love can be—holding hands
in the spring meadow

the daisies
you paint   full
of philosophy

the night you tell me
the diagnosis—starlight
skids down icicles

slimmer each time
I come   your brushes still
plump with pictures

so dark, you say
one bright day, the room full
of narcissus

blind, you feel
canvas edges, cover one
with color   like petals

reading to you
you stop me to listen
to owl tints

your lover
cradling you at the last—
full autumn moon

mountaintop—
we offer your ashes
to wind and weeds

just bird anthems
as we watch fine dust
through filmed eyes

one-man show:
the depth of you everywhere—
I arrange chrysanthemums

I hold your lover—
speechless, we say our love
to Venus rising

from *Star-Mapped*

WOMAN IN A SPECIAL HOUSE

*W*hite birds come often to this beach where my small house holds its own far back from the water. Three of the birds are familiar, with a certain distinction about them. That is not to say I could with confidence call them gulls or terns. They're more exotic than either. They make a murmuring noise, though they are not roosting.

This morning I am dancing. One bird has flown off towards the brilliantly russet sun. I am inspired to try *Swan Lake*. I put on the cassette of the Philadelphia Orchestra under Ricardo Muti's direction. Muti is enchanting in that intense Italian way. And he's masterful with Russian music.

I find an old costume belonging to my sister. She's married and lives in California now. The feathers are bedraggled and bits of them whirl off as I dance, but what matter? My partner is Diaghilev in his heyday. There's never been any dancer like Diaghilev, *I* think. Stern and innovative, stunningly agile, marvelous looking, I am sure he always kissed ladies' hands.

After our pas de deux I sit down to rest, am shadowed a moment by one of the birds. It eases away and I think about Tschaikowsky and Von Meck. All those years of correspondence. flow unsatisfying. But look what they produced. If I were not ever to offer my body to Charles again, would I produce anything for the ages? Would he?

Where is Charles, anyway? Is he annoyed because he likes lakes, not oceans? This comes up every summer.

"What about a little place at the ocean, Charles, this year? There's the boardwalk, evenings, and I love to fight the breakers, love to try to get out beyond them where there are just great swells."

"God save me from boardwalks." Charles holds his head. "For a woman of culture you have feet of clay."

I don't bother to straighten *that* out, for he gets annoyed if I nit-pick about English.

So, one year we go to the lake and one year to the ocean. I have to admit, except for the water (I hate lake water, all those strange, slimy, weedy things under the surface), Charles is right. The boardwalk, all boardwalks, are insults. We take a place at a beach without any boardwalk, finally, and just occasionally drive to the next town, with boardwalk, if we feel desperate enough to want grinding noise, deafening music, shuffling people, salt-water taffy machines, and the oddest T-shirts I've ever seen.

"We might as well always go to the lake, Laura, where there is peace, quiet, and stars that come and sit on your shoulders."

"Mm—yes," I say, pulling at my lip. I love those things. But once in a while I like to slum and not have to drive one hundred miles to the nearest movie. Too, one simply mustn't give in so easily. A woman must take stands, must hang on to certain things as if they were life preservers, which in fact they may be.

So I don't really mean the "yes." Charles knows that, surely he does.

Here there is the immense ocean with its swells you can lie on, dream on. I forget Tschaikowsky, his homosexual anguish, and race to the shore, push past the breakers, and let myself go on one grand swell. How lovely, how bodiless I am, how otherworldly.

There is a white bird over me, again. It is dipping very near. It is immense. I am frightened. I cry out. It backs off. It is staring at me; it stares for a long, long time. I do not like its sharp purplish eyes.

What does it want of me?

I run back to my house, my feet ice cold, even on the burning sand. I sit in a corner of the living room and pull the *Swan Lake* costume over my eyes.

But you can't hide behind a costume forever. The bird is nowhere in sight now, I see, inching from behind the ragged tutu. I am alone in this house; it is very cold.

I want Charles. We have been married ten years. We have no children, can't have them. We've decided to adopt. We've already started negotiations for a Colombian boy and girl. I am thrilled, more, I am deeply satisfied in some center of myself. We will bring them to the shore. Charles will make one of the sandcastles he builds as if he were creating one of the great chateaux of France. Or Buckingham Palace, maybe. He takes endless pains and time. People come to look at his work, astonished. It is the one thing about the beach that he adores.

"A pity the tide will wash it all away," I am always moved to comment.

"The fun is in the making of it." Charles smiles in his easy way. The sun has made his faun-colored hair almost blond. Normally angular, he has put on rounding pounds in our lolling, swimming, eating, reading, lazy vacation life.

Yes, he will make our children wonderful castles. We will all walk and gather shells. We will explain to them, carefully, what each one is. We always bring with us books on birds, shells, trees, frustrated if we can't know what the world is about.

I sit at the window of my house, across which straggles a vine-like weed, like veins across my eyes. I don't recognize the weed and am about to get the book when the bird comes back with another bird. I haven't seen this one before; it has feathers green as jade. I shudder, afraid, as they come close to me.

Then I see.

I see what they are.

"It's been six months, doctor. Nothing. Not a flicker. Not even when her husband comes in."

Not even when her husband comes in.

"No, no," I shout. "Charles hasn't come. I keep wondering where he is."

"A little tremor of her left hand. that's all," the green birdman says, bending over me. "A terrible thing. Beautiful young woman, everything to live for. Hope they jail the guy that hit her in that alley, for a long, long time."

"What are you talking about? Tell me, tell me. Charles, where are you?"

"Trouble is, they're out of jail in no time, these days." My white nursebird tucks covers round my feet. "Do you suppose the family will petition to take her off the respirator, doctor, eventually?"

God, my God. I am *alive*.

"Much too soon even to think about that, nurse, though in this case... it tears you apart, no matter how often you see it."

"Yes, sure does." The white bird raises one wing to a bottle over my head.

"Listen," I scream. "*I can hear you.* Can't you hear me? Listen, please listen."

"The hand tremor has stopped. Just keep her as comfortable as possible, nurse, though she can't feel anything."

"You're wrong, terribly wrong." I have never shrilled so loud before in my life. "This morning I felt my feet dancing; it was quite wonderful. I was listening to Tschaikowsky, was thinking about how many years he wrote to Von Meck. *Listen.* I was swimming, was gathering shells, was waiting for Charles, thinking about being in bed with him...."

The nursebird comes to adjust the dinosaur that puffs beside me.

"Have you children?" I shriek. "A husband? Don't you understand...."

She flies away.

I know now that I must hoard all energy, all thought, towards plotting how to get out.

This is just a house. I must batter down these doors, break these windows, tear away all weeds. The thin wisp of my breath, so like a silken thread that tethers me to Charles, to Muti, to Diaghilev, to my children, must go on.

Enormous black clouds of wild, wild birds beat in me, pecking, scratching, squawking. Summoning great sharp whips from the storehouse of me, I bat them away. I must bang, kick, fist at the doors, the windows. Houses can be broken, even the sturdiest.

I cannot yet get to the ocean, cannot get past the breakers to the lovely mauve-azure buoyant water that would hold me, to the swells that would carry me lightly, lightly, everywhere, anywhere.

No. Not yet. But I can hear, beyond the crashing, foaming breakers, the sounds in the falling swells. Fish turn, lazily, lithely, in silvery bodies, telling old tales. Seaweeds amble to, fro, to, fro, full of syllables retrieved from the shores they've touched. Shells tumble on deep sands like children somersaulting, cartwheeling; they murmur and laugh. Crabs, lobsters tell me of ancient places, remarkable waters.

I am not alone in this house.

All creatures and things of the sea whisper, whisper, their long poems of survival.

I am in touch with whatever I need to swim, strongly.

Soon the white birds and the green birds will wear the silken shawls I have made for them, of my ongoing breath.

They will understand that they are prayer-shawls they must not discard.

Listen, you can hear me weaving from the depths of the earliest seas.

In a moment, this very moment, I am going to dance again. This time to the immense important swells of *La Mer*.

from *Woman in a Special House*

172

CONTEMPLATIONS

hospital mate
delirious at three a.m.,
I think of wild roses

stuck for blood again
the deep burgundy
of my climbing rose

unable to eat
I sip orange juice smooth
as rose petals

home again—
the one pale ivory rose
my "rude" neighbor brings...

watching a windswirl
of pink rose petals outside
before paying bills

sleepless though sleepy
I open the rose catalog,
begin to count blooms

no, wouldn't smell
as sweet by other name,
I muse, sleepy at last

in dreams
a rose is a rose unfolding
from bud and thorns

Unpublished

MAPLE

So this is what pain is, the harsh drone
of a saw tearing off limbs you tell me
are cancerous even to death. What can we believe?

Here are leaves like kaleidoscope chips
flung from the wounded mother, settling
on the porch unmasked by lack
of fifty-year shadows. I gather an armful
of hues on fire. Nothing to do with fall
just pressing towards winter.
I think if I shake them
three boys in ripped jeans will shinny up
to the chuckle of robins ordering the world again
to beginnings. A squirrel will scatter bees
they may or may not avoid as they climb
towards the top and believe they are conquering
everything, forever. To the left a hawk
slides slow circles far above bulbs
showing bits of breast to the rain
not yet hurrying the climber's descent.

Shake and they're tall, tall
spinning up trees academic and corporate,
scattered like leaves I clutch
as if I could hold
in the kaleidoscope's circle
always
children in the perfect tree
nothing could grind
to dust.

from *A Well-Tuned Harp*

how bright the sound
of one star humming
among the many

from *Star-Mapped*

GERALDINE CLINTON LITTLE: BIBLIOGRAPHY

The Ballad of Loner Jim: the Saga of a Sniper. Limited edition, 1976.

Separation: Seasons in Space. West Lafayette, IN: Sparrow Press, 1979

Contrasts in Keening: Ireland. Hainesport, NJ: Silver Apples Press, 1982.

Hakugai: Poem from a Concentration Camp. Austin, TX: Curbstone Publishing, 1983.

Endless Waves. Westfield, NJ: Merging Media, 1984.

The Spinalonga Poems. Glen Burnie, MD: A Wind Chimes Minibook, 1986.

Strong Against the Frost. Hainesport, NJ: Green Glens Press, 1986.

Beyond the Boxwood Comb: Six Women's Voices from Japan. West Lafayette, IN: Sparrow Press, 1988.

A Well-Tuned Harp. Upper Montclair, NJ: Saturday Press, 1988.

Heloise and Abelard: A Verse Play: Ecstasies & Adversities. Lanham, MD: University Press of America: 1989.

Star-Mapped. Hainesport, NJ: Silver Apples Press, 1989.

Bluestones and Salt Hay: An Anthology of Contemporary New Jersey Poets. Edited by Joel Lewis. New Brunswick, NJ: Rutgers University Press, 1990.

"Women: In the Mask and Beyond." *Quarterly Review of Literature: Poetry Series.* Princeton, NJ: Quarterly Review of Literature Poetry Series, Volume XXX, 1991.

More Light, Larger Vision. Gualala, CA: AHA Books, 1992.

Ministries. San Diego, CA: Crazy Quilt Press, 1992.

Out of Darkness. Lanham, MD: University Press of America, 1993.

No Home to Return to But This. Canton, OH: Singular Speech Press, 1994.

Molded Out of Faults. Huntington, WV: University Editions, 1997.

Woman in a Special House, and Other Stories. Santa Barbara, CA: Fithian Press, 1997.

Contemplations. La Crosse, WI: Juniper Press, 1997.

UNPUBLISHED

"Travelers of Eternity," manuscript of poems

"Contemplations and Bell Tones," manuscript of poems

"The Desert Shall Rejoice," memoir of her mother

"Toward Healing," a poem